The Author

William P. Tuck is pastor of the First Baptist Church, Bristol, Virginia. He is also serving as adjunct professor of religion at Virginia Intermont College. Previous pastorates have been in Louisiana and Virginia. In both states he has been active in civic and denominational work.

A native of Virginia, Dr. Tuck is a graduate of the University of Richmond (B.A.), Southeastern Baptist Seminary (Th.M.), and New Orleans Baptist Seminary (Th.D.), plus graduate study at Emory University. Although this is his first book, he has had articles published in a number of magazines.

Facing Grief AND Death

Facing Grief AND Death

William P. Tuck

BROADMAN PRESS / Nashville, Tennessee

Kansas-Nebraska Convention of Southern Baptists

© Copyright 1975 • Broadman Press

All rights reserved

4224-09

ISBN: 0-8054-2409-1

Library of Congress Catalog Card Number: 75-2977

Dewey Decimal Classification: 242.4

Printed in the United States of America

Preface

Life can be a most exciting, creative, wondrous, enthusiastic adventure or it can be a journey which is filled only with despair, pessimism, hopelessness, and depression. Our perspective towards life and death makes all the difference in the world. These pages are not written to encourage anyone to put on rose-colored glasses but are directed, hopefully, to challenge a realistic view of life. Death is a part of life which no one can avoid or escape. We may try to ignore it or disguise it, but it will still not go away. We must learn how to live with death—our own and others' whom we love.

In Eric Marshall and Stuart Hample's book *Children's Letters to God*, a young boy writes: "Dear God, What is it like when you die. Nobody will tell me. I just want to know, I don't want to do it. Your friend, Mike." The child's question is the age-old question of the sages. What is death all about? How do you make sense of life with the death vulture always hovering overhead? How do you have courage to face death and its meaning? For face it we must. We are mortal.

In recent years death has taken a large number from our church congregation. Many of these were older members who had been strong leaders in church and community; some were young people who died before they reached maturity; and others were men and women in the prime of life. It is to these families that I have ministered, and from them I have learned much as I shared their grief.

The depth and extent of this grief led me to conclude that the problem needed to be faced by our whole congregation. In an effort to help our people prepare themselves for grief and death, we participated in a study entitled "Living with Dying." Included in this study were the messages found in Part I, which have been expanded in this volume, and the forum of speakers (Part II) who presented a brief discussion of death from their particular perspectives—medical, teaching, legal, and funereal. Following their presentations I usually directed some questions to them which began a period of dialogue with the congregation.

The selections in Part II were taped while they were presented and have been edited only to make them more readable and precise. In places, I wish some of the speakers had said more. I also differ with the speakers on some points, but the feeling is doubtless mutual. In any case there is no study where one can agree with all conclusions. As a whole, I feel the presentations in Part II will provide some much needed guidelines which I have not seen touched on any place else. I appreciate the gracious manner in which each of the participants shared in this study.

The following participated in the forum on death: Dr. H. Douglas Lee, Director of University Relations, Wake Forest University and formerly Professor of Religion and Philosophy at Virginia Intermont College, Bristol, Virginia, examines death from a teacher's perspective. Dr. Claude H. Crockett, Jr., a physician in Bristol, Tennessee, looks at death from the medical viewpoint. Mr. Paul Cook, Jr., a funeral director in Bristol, Tennessee, speaks of the funeral and death. The legal questions about death are probed by Mr. Albert B. Cooper, Jr., who is engaged in the private practice of law in Bristol, Virginia.

I want to express appreciation to Miss Joann Feazell for typing the manuscript through several drafts. She completed this task after a period of personal bereavement and indicated that the manuscript was helpful to her in working through her own grief. I am indebted to Dr. Gordon Kingsley, Associate Dean of William Jewell College, and Dr. Paul D. Simmons, Assistant Professor of Ethics at Southern Baptist Theological Seminary, who read the manuscript and offered many valuable suggestions. To my wife, Emily Campbell Tuck, I am deeply grateful for her continued counsel, stimulating criticisms, and insights.

Death is not a subject which many people find very comfortable to think about or talk about, but we must do both. When we have both thought and talked about death, then maybe, as the late Carl Michalson said, we will be "free from the fear of death because our life is lived toward our own erosive future." [1]

To the memory of
PAUL M. CAMPBELL
who taught me much
about living and dying

Contents

1
The Fear of Death

In George Seaton's film *The Proud and the Profane*, the steps of a young nurse are traced to Iwo Jima where her husband had been killed in World War II. She goes to the cemetery where her husband lies buried and turns to the caretaker, a shell-shocked soldier, who had seen her husband die. "How did he die?" she asked. "Like an amateur," he replies. "They teach you how to hurl a grenade and how to fire a mortar, but nobody teaches you how to die. There are no professionals in dying."

Isn't it ironical that in an age when man has been exposed to violence and death on such a massive scale, he has nevertheless not considered very deeply the reality of death. Death cannot be easily evaded in an age which has moved through gas chambers, concentration camps, atomic holocaust, global wars, slaughter on the highways, mass starvation, riots, and violence to say nothing of earthquakes, volcanic eruptions, floods, avalanches, blizzards, and other natural disasters. Everyone has experienced death in one way or another—the loss of a parent, a child, a brother or sister, a husband or a wife, or a friend. If we have not experienced this loss already, one day soon we shall. The psalmist has reflected our predicament, "What man can live and never see death?" (Ps. 89:48). Death is a reality which confronts all men, and no one can avoid its disturbing presence on the path of daily living. "Every man's death diminishes me," John Donne reminds us. Therefore, when we hear the church bell tolling, we need to "Ask not . . . it tolls for thee."

With the experience of so much dying around us, one would think that man by now would know how to face death with less futility and struggle. But there are still "no professionals in dying." The fear of death remains the paramount fear of all men.

Death-Denying Practices

Why doesn't man know how to die? He clings in part to what Morris West has called "the illusion of immortality." We are unable to face the certainty of our own death. Like the priest in West's novel *The Devil's Advocate*, who learns he has only a few months to live, we continue to live with our denial of death. "He was a reasonable man and reason told him that a man's death sentence is written on his palm the day he is born; he was a cold man, little troubled by passion, irked not at all by discipline, yet his first impulse had been a wild clinging to the illusion of immortality." [1]

Scientific and medical progress has contributed to our illusion. Epidemics and infant mortality once inflicted a heavy loss in the population. Improved medicine, mass vaccinations, the availability of medical services and staff, and better living conditions have helped eradicate much illness and infectious diseases. Who doesn't cling to the hope that science or medicine will have the answer to his health problems and death will be escaped again. Sigmund Freud noted that everyone is basically convinced of his own immortality. We live as though death did not exist for us. We can acknowledge the death of others, but our own is beyond imagination. The seventeenth-century French writer, La Rochefoucauld, was accurate when he said, "One can no more look steadily at death than at the sun."

We cling to the illusion that if we just eat the right food, if we get enough rest and sleep, if we get the proper exercise, if we take the correct medications, if we get the proper medical attention, death will not creep into our lives. Of course all of us know that death cannot ultimately be denied, as helpful as all these may be to prolong life. We live each day under a death sentence, as it were. King Philip of Macedon, the father of Alexander the Great, had a slave whose task was to remind the king every morning, "Philip, remember that you must die." Philip was trying to face death as a genuine, real part of life. No one is fully able to face life until he has learned to face the reality of his own death. "Making sense of life," J. S. Whale observes, "means, ultimately and always, making sense of Death." [2] Whether life is viewed as absurd or meaningful is determined by one's view of the ending of it.

Not only can we not accept our own death but we try to deny its reality by disguising and camouflaging it. If the maxim of Marshall McLuhan, "The medium is the message," is correct, then the way we hide and veil death reveals far more about our real understanding of death than anything else. Instead of saying someone has died, we employ euphemisms of all kinds. Our very words to escape the word "death" attempt to disguise death and make it appear unreal when we say: "he has passed on," "she has passed away," "he has departed," "she is asleep," "he has gone home," or "he has expired."

Jessica Mitford's book *The American Way of Death* denounces many of the funeral practices in our country in their expensive and elaborate manner of denying death. But we cannot get off the hook so easily by blaming the funeral directors alone. Are they not depicting what many of us want? We want death camou flaged. We feel more comfortable around the dead when death has been made to appear unreal or artificial; when it is concealed cosmetically; when it is made sweet and soft by satin, pillows, and flowers. The body is disguised to appear asleep and look younger. We put the obituaries in small print so they can be ignored. The medium is indeed the message! We fear death so much we will go almost to any extreme to deny it and conceal it.

Our methods of disguising death and the use of euphemism are merely attempts to ignore death. We want to push it out of our minds. Death has replaced sex as the new taboo subject in modern society. At the same time, violent death has become the subject of a new type of pornographic literature and films.[3] We ignore death in our table and street conversation and, at the same moment, filmmakers exploit sex, death, and violence as a means of escape and "entertainment."

I can still remember the reaction of a woman in a former church when I dropped by to talk to her about the death of a relative. As she came into the room, she quickly ushered the children out of the room and informed me that she did not want to discuss "the passing away" of Aunt Blank. She made it clear that she did not go to funerals, would not let her children attend them, or be around any discussion of death. To her it was a morbid subject and something you just did not discuss.

Many people have become sick emotionally and physically because of an attempt to ignore death. Counselors have found, on the other hand, that a healthy facing of death has brought about a reduction in inner tension instead of distorting life. Some of our colleges are now offering courses in thanatology in which death, the process of dying, and one's own funeral are discussed freely in vivid detail. The courses are becoming some of the most popular courses on campuses. Maybe the next generation will approach death with more openness.

Some of our death-denying practices have been introduced only in more recent years. The generation of my grandparents were more familiar with death. My father-in-law lived to be in his late seventies and was himself the youngest of thirteen children. I can remember hearing him tell on several occasions about the death of his own father. His father had been a farmer and when he became critically ill, he remained at home to die in his own bed. He called each child in, one by one, and talked to them about his death and his hopes for them. When he died, he was buried by his own family and friends in a plot of land on his own property which he had chosen for the family cemetery. What needed to be done, his family did. Then they shared their grief together. They faced the reality of his death without any cosmetics.

Most of us do not want to go back to the time where the

family had to handle all of the details of burying the dead. Never-theless, the generation that handled personally their dead loved ones seemed to have far less fears and unconscious anxieties about death than the present generation. Our very unwillingness to live with dying is a frightful indication of something vital which is absent from our lives. "The man who loves life lives a fuller and better life," Felix Marti-Ibanez once said, "because he has put death in its proper place."

Karl Barth, considered by many to be one of this century's greatest theologians, has observed: "The man who takes seriously and seizes his unique opportunity differs from the one who does not by reason of the fact that he always remembers he will die and yet never fears death. We have no option but to say that this is the central and decisive criterion from the standpoint of Christian theology." [4] Psychiatrists have observed that the fear of death is probably the central anxiety of all our fears.

Responses to an Awareness of Death

What is man's reaction when the knowledge of his own death is disclosed to him? People respond to this awareness in different ways. *Some react with despair.* They simply give up. One woman I know, when told she had cancer and would not recover, shut herself up in her house and waited to die. "I never want to see anybody or anything again," she declared. Although not an invalid, she gave in to despair. A stroke patient turned within himself, away from his family, friends, and physician and refused all help and support.

Others lash out in rage against death. Like the German philosopher Nietzsche, some curse death and rage in defiance against the finality of death. Rather than face death with abject resignation, man is challenged with all his being to overcome death. I remember a teenage friend of mine who had leukemia asserting, "I will not die; I will beat this stuff." But he did not. Dylan Thomas' poem "Do Not Go Gentle into That Good Night" has voiced well man's struggle against death.

Instead of defiance, *some project a type of hedonistic philosophy.*

Well, if I'm going to die soon, I'll have a last fling. "Eat, drink and be merry for tomorrow you die." One attempts to gorge himself with all the pleasures of the moment. Occasionally when one learns that he may face death within a short period of time, such as a few months or within a year, *the desire to live dangerously* is overwhelming. The television series *Run for Your Life*, starring Ben Gazarra, depicted a young man who knew he would die within a year. In the series he participated in a variety of dangerous episodes. This may seem unrealistic to most of us, but how often has a wounded soldier completed heroic tasks and sometimes saved the lives of many of his comrades by his courageous deeds, when he knew that certain death was only minutes away from him personally?

Sometimes on learning of his approaching death, a person determines that he will *embrace it in the present and not wait.* Living has become more difficult than dying; life seems more horrible than death; waiting appears more anxiety ridden than losing life. Suicide often becomes an option for more than we would like to imagine. How often I have heard severely ill patients say: "I wish I could die." "Why doesn't God take me?" "I hope I go to sleep and do not wake up." "I can't go on without him (or her). Life is empty for me now." When I was a student in seminary, a feeling of shock and disbelief swept across the campus when word was received that one of the professors had shot himself. The stillness in the chapel was heavy as the students gathered for the memorial service to honor one whom they had loved. Rather than wait for cancer to end his life slowly, the professor chose to terminate his own life.

Still others have learned of their impending death and have selected to *commit the remaining time,* whether days, weeks, or months, to accomplish the most good possible in the short period of time. Dr. Tom Dooley, who gave his life as a medical doctor to help the underprivileged in Southeast Asia, learned that he himself was dying with cancer. He returned to Southeast Asia, however, and gave his medical skill and love to those poor people as long as he was able. A young seminary student, learning of his terminal illness, shared with others through his writings and conversation the inner faith and courage which enabled him to accept the reality of his own death.

Man reacts to the knowledge of his own death in a varied fashion. Some despair; others rage; some become playboys or attempt to live dangerously; a few choose suicide; still others face it with a sense of commitment of life and use the last few days courageously and with service.

Fears About Death

Everyone has some conscious or unconscious fears about death. Books we have read; movies or television programs we have watched; accounts related to us about the way someone else died; our personal experience with the dying—all of these and others contribute to our fears, uncertainties, and anxieties about death. Let us examine some of the more common fears that all of us face.

One of the most universal fears is that our dying may be filled with *pain and suffering*. How often we hear an elderly person say: "I do not fear death itself so much as the process of dying. I am so fearful that I will have to endure a long period of suffering." No one can say that this may not be the case, but it is far less likely today with all the medications of modern science. Physical suffering, or at least the awareness of it, by the dying patient has been greatly diminished. Dr. William Osler made a study in the 1880's of five hundred dying patients and observed that only ninety were actually suffering physical pain. Nevertheless, if we were one of the ninety, or if one of our loved ones were, it would not lessen the pain.

God has not promised us that we would never suffer or have pain. He does not deliberately send suffering or will it upon us, but he does allow its existence in his world. Why? There is no final answer to that question. We do know that he did not evade it even for himself but allowed his own Son to be rejected and crucified by men. The promise from God is not the deliverance from all pain and suffering but the assurance that his presence abides in the midst of any situation. Nothing ultimately can separate us from his love, not even death itself.

Another common fear is that our dying may take on an *impersonal nature* to those administering to our needs. No one wants to become merely an object or a "thing" being treated. Some express a real fear that the dying process may make them only a body to be cared for and kept alive by tubes and machines. The fear expressed here is the fear of the loss of personhood. The dying patient often feels stripped of all his rights as a genuine human being. His opinion is no longer considered significant, and others whisper around him as they make all the decisions for him. Ill as the patient may be, he does not want to suffer the additional indignity of being ignored as a person without the right to some decisions about his own destiny.

Elizabeth Kübler-Ross in her book *On Death and Dying* declares that the question is not whether you *should* tell a person that he is dying but *how*.[5] She found that when the dying patient was informed of his condition and allowed to be a part of the conversing community about it, he was able to confront his fears about death and relate better to all around him.

The *fear of oblivion* at death is a feeling shared by many. "I fear," the patient said, "that death will simply be the end of my personal existence. I will not exist any more." Contemporary man echoes this hidden fear in his various means of avoiding conversation or thoughts about death. Shakespeare's play *Hamlet* is a struggle with the question of death and existence, and Hamlet's meditation, "To be or not to be?" has become parabolic of every man's quest for meaning and existence. "To be or not to be?" This is the question that death raises before our eyes. Does death terminate my existence as a person? Is my life so tied to the physical body that when it dies that's all there is? But the Christian affirms with the apostle Paul that it is sown a physical body but raised a spiritual body: sown a mortal body, raised an immortal body. Christians walk in the presence of a living Lord and in the assurance of life everlasting.

The *fear of separation* is a repeated anxiety about death. No one wants to leave loved ones, children, parents, a husband, or a wife. We enjoy the sense of togetherness and mutual love and trust. This is a natural feeling, and we would all be poorer without it. I have heard the question on many occasions, "Will we know each other in the life after death?" The answer has to be yes. What kind of existence or life would it be without recognition of loved ones and friends? At the transfiguration of Jesus, the disciples recognized Moses and Elijah. The disciples also knew Jesus after the resurrection. This fear can be overcome by the awareness that whatever awaits man, God will be just and meaningful. "Beloved, we are God's children now; it does not yet appear what we shall be. For we know that if he be manifested we shall be like him, for we shall see him just as he is" (1 John 3:2).

The possibility of *being a burden* to others is a fear with which many of us live. I do not know of anyone who is willing to talk about his dying who does not say: "When I die, I hope I go quickly." "I do not want to linger and suffer a long time. I don't want someone else to wait on me. I don't want to be a burden to my family." Many of us have had relatives, or have known friends who have had them, who were virtually helpless and had to be taken care of like a baby or a semi-invalid for years. The care, financial obligation, strain, physical labor, and emotionally draining effort may be devastating to all involved. Mixed feelings surface within family members as they seek to meet the needs of such a person. We are often torn between tenderness and repulsion, sympathy and pity, love and hate, concern and guilt. The fear of becoming a burden to others is understandable. There is no such thing, however, as a completely independent person.

We all need and depend on others at various stages in our lives. When we were small we were absolutely dependent on our parents. Now our children are dependent upon us. We were reminded of this truth during a three-year-confinement of my father-in-law following a stroke. Our family learned to share our gift of love and care for him. While healthy, he had shared the gift of his love and concern for us. Ordinarily he was a very independent person, but during his disability he had to discover

the other side of giving, the ability to accept. Sometimes it is
easier for us to give than receive, but a part of life is learning
how to accept the love and support of others who care for us
deeply.

We who have given must also be willing to accept the love
of others. Rejection would be the only other alternative. Halford
Luccock expressed this point clearly: "It is more blessed to give
than to receive. . . . The givers who cannot take in return miss
one of the finest graces in life, the grace of receiving. . . . To
receive gratefully from others is to enhance others' sense of their
worth. It puts them on a give-and-take level, the only level on
which real fellowship can be sustained. . . . It changes one of
the ugliest things in the world, patronage, into one of the richest
things in the world, friendship." [6]

Some of us fear that death may leave our *work unfinished or
our goals unfulfilled*. We fear that we may not see our children
grow up, marry, and raise families of their own. We may fear
that we will not complete the goals and aspirations which we
have set for our lives. At the death of Dr. A. M. Fairbairn, Principal
of Oxford, theologian, philosopher, and English professor, his
family and friends discovered memos which he had left in his
office of work he intended to do which would have taken him
three hundred years to accomplish. Yet he had lived to an old
age. Do any of us ever fully realize all our goals? New tasks
continue to meet us; new responsibilities confront us; new opportunities beckon as long as we are open and growing.

Recently my wife received a letter from one of her aunts who
is 84 years old. This lovely, gracious lady has a home in which
she takes care of *old* people. One of the ladies she cares for is
101. In her letter she said: "I love life and there are many things
I must accomplish yet, not for myself but for so many people
who are in great need to understand God's love and the strength
he provides for each day." Here is represented a youthful vision
of tasks yet to be done. No matter what age a person is, there
are still dreams, hopes, aspirations, desires, wishes, potential which
want to be realized. The Christian affirms, however, that death

does not finalize our opportunity for growth but opens before us a new dimension for fulfillment in the deeper resources of God's presence.

Death still looms before us all as the great *unknown*. We like to have our feet stationed on firm soil; we want all the answers to our questions; we long for certainties; we are afraid of guesses; and faith does not seem as secure as actual, visual knowledge. Like a small child preparing to go to summer camp, we are fearful of leaving the safe, familiar surroundings of home. If we could just know for sure, the fear of death would not linger over us so fiercely. Christian knowledge is on a different plane. It entails commitment and trust; our assurance is a Living Presence; our hope is in a redeeming love.

Facing Our Fears of Death

In the awareness of our fear of death how do we confront this anxiety? *First, we must learn to face our fear and not hide from it.* The fear of death can become a phobia which is so strong that it fills much of our living with irrational responses. Augustine stated in his *Confessions* that it is only in the facing of death that man's self is born. Freud observed that if you would endure life, be prepared for death. The Christian seeks to do more than just endure life, but he is aware that genuine living has already anticipated the reality of death. In recounting his lifelong struggle to gain victory over his old enemy rheumatic heart disease, H. C. Brown, Jr., stated that a friend shared with him his helpful philosophy for attacking fears: "The way to defeat your fear is to walk toward it." This message helped to change his life, and in his book *Walking Toward Your Fear* Dr. Brown shared with us how this lesson enabled him to overcome his fears.[7] The anxiety about death can be lessened by facing it honestly and openly within ourselves and with our family and friends.

Secondly, we face our fear of death by learning to accept *life as a gift*. Life comes to each of us as a great gift of God. Life is not something we have earned, merited, deserved, or even anticipated, but it was given to us as a free gift by the gracious creativity of God. Out of his boundless love God made life and gave its gift to us. We have the opportunity to embrace it and enjoy it to its fullness or waste it and misuse the gift.

Last summer when we were at the ocean I played with my children in the sand, and we built sand castles with detailed windows, doors, bridges, and moats. When we concluded our play, the children took delight in knocking down the towers, walls, and bridges and allowing the water to sweep over our creation until it looked as though it had never existed. God's gift of life to us is not like that. That which God has given to us out of his love will not be ended by the sweeping hand of death. God's love continues to give everlasting life to the Christian which not even death itself will ultimately destroy. John tells us, "And this is eternal life, that they know thee the only true God, and Jesus Christ whom thou hast sent" (John 17:3). Eternal life for the Christian is a present reality which not even death is able to remove. What God has made, he intends to keep.

Thirdly, we face our *fear of death with the assurance of the presence of Christ.* Jesus Christ was no stranger to the fear of death. He faced this same fear in the garden of Gethsemane and as he hung alone on the cross. He approached death like we do: only by faith in his Father's love and not by a money-back guarantee. Carlyle Marney has said it forcefully:

Even the Christ had to faith his way through death. Who would refuse to die for the sins of the world for three days if he knew he would rise? He faithed his way; he pulled no rank on us. The heresy of our time is not that we preached Christ as if he were not God; it is, rather, that we preached Jesus as if he were not man. He faithed that the purpose of God would bring him through, and the Christian faith hangs on what the Father did! [8]

Christ approached death as you and I do, by faith, and his faith blossomed into the reality of the resurrection. The early church asserted its faith from the presence of the risen Christ who proclaimed, "Because I live, you will live also" (John 14:19). Montaigne is correct: "Only the man who no longer fears death has ceased to be a slave." Jesus Christ sets us free from the phobia of death. May we learn to echo with John Donne these words:

> Death, be not proud, though some have called thee
> Mighty and dreadful, for thou art not so:
> For those whom thou think'st thou dost overthrow
> Die not, poor Death; not yet canst thou kill me.
> From rest and sleep, which but thy picture be,
> Much pleasure, then from thee much more must flow;
> And soonest our best men with thee do go—
> Rest of their bones and souls' delivery
> Thou'rt slave to fate, chance, kings, and desperate men,
> And dost with poison, war, and sickness dwell;
> And poppy or charms can make us sleep as well
> And better than thy stroke. Why swell'st thou then?
> One short sleep past, we wake eternally,
> And Death shall be no more: Death, thou shalt die! [9]

2
Learning How to Meet Grief

Faces of grief crowd into my memory; they are not quickly or easily forgotten. The teenage couple sat beside the open grave. The day was biting cold with the temperature standing slightly above zero. A heavy snow covered the ground. Only four of us were present: the young couple, the funeral director and I, and one tiny casket containing a six-month-old child. Clinging to each other by the graveside, the young couple sobbed pitifully. The tiny baby had smothered to death in its crib. Their grief was overpowering, and they expressed it openly. The young couple was not married. Their parents and friends did not even know of the birth, much less the death of the infant. Alone, away from friends, they struggled with the reality of grief.

Another face appears . . . The young man was just back from the Vietnam War and his ambition was to be an FBI agent. Strong, alert, highly motivated, with a vision for service and work, he had survived the jungles of Southeast Asia only to be killed in a head-on automobile crash near Washington, D. C. Another face emerges . . . The young boy's future was bright with promise. With his keen mind, he loved to raise difficult questions and was constantly pushing one to the limit of his ability to furnish answers and directions to the most profound questions and issues. But the light of his inquiry was lost from among us as he stepped from behind a bus at a football game into the path of an oncoming car.

Yet another appears . . . Each Sunday the young couple sat near the front of the church. Their beautiful, little nine-year-old, blond-haired daughter was always between them. She was the joy of their lives. Suddenly the ugly hand of leukemia removed her from their lives. Many other faces of grief rush into my mind; so many are they and so varied.

Most of us have sat by the bedside of a parent, a child, a husband or wife, a friend—someone we loved who is now gone, and we, too, have memories of grief which flood our mind. Grief is real; it is no illusion. No one walks the earth and escapes it. How do you face grief and the memories which it brings? How do you meet the dark night of sorrow which sooner or later touches every home and every life? Each of us searches for what Joshua Liebman has described as "the slow wisdom of grief." To be resolved or lessened, grief must be confronted. Few of us are aware of what to expect when the pain of grief touches us.

Physical and Psychological Reactions

Whenever my children have to go see a doctor or a dentist, they always want to know in advance, "Will it hurt?" No child likes to be surprised by the sharp thrust of a needle or taste a bitter medicine when they expect a pleasant flavor. We as parents are no different. We want to know if the inoculation or prescription will have any reaction. We would rather have the doctor tell us that we may feel feverish or sleepy or tired from the medication than be affected without prior alertness to the possibility. Someone needs to forewarn us of the probable physical and psychological reactions which may happen to us in a grief experience.

"No one ever told me that grief felt so like fear," wrote C. S. Lewis after the death of his wife. "I am not afraid, but the sensation is like being afraid. The same fluttering in the stomach, the same restlessness, the yawning. I keep on swallowing." [1]

In grief mixed feelings overtake us. Erich Lindemann of Harvard Medical School [2] and others have noted that one often feels a physical pain in the chest, an ache in the abdomen, a ceaseless throbbing in the head, nausea and faintness, dryness in the mouth and a tightness in the throat, choking and shortness of breath, a lack of power in the muscles, palpitation of the heart, followed sometimes by chills and tremors. The grief sufferer may also have feelings of distress, tension, and loneliness, or seem tired and weary. Objects may seem heavy. The sufferer may have a loss of appetite or sense a need to sigh; he may have a sinking feeling or a sense of being empty within; he may not be able to determine reality. He may also become irritable or hostile.

Most people are not aware that these feelings are perfectly normal reactions which we may experience in our time of grief. An iceberg is only about one-sixth visible above the water; the larger approximately five-sixths is invisible and below the surface. Our real feelings may be those which are not seen on the surface but are buried iceberg-like within us. No matter what mask we may attempt to wear in our response to grief, the invisible, buried psychological factors may be those which determine our real reactions.

The adjustment to grief is a slow, difficult process, and the physical and psychological reactions may increase and become more pronounced over a period of a few days or weeks. The busy, modern world allows little time for grief and one's recovery from its shock. So often people are forced by society to handle their bereavement quickly, which often suppresses or pushes it inward instead of meeting and dealing with it.

Grief pulls us in different directions. We experience conflicting feelings of faith and doubt, trust and anxiety, peace and anger, blamelessness and guilt, calm and shock, memories and dreams, hopes and cares, confidence and depression, and many others. Nevertheless, if we have a prior awareness that we may feel a certain way physically or emotionally in bereavement, it can ease the mind from needless worry or the foolish notion that our feelings or bodily sensations are not normal. Any normal person will grieve, but the Christian seeks to affirm: "Grieve not as others do who have no hope" (1 Thess. 4:13).

Normal Stages of Grief

Erich Lindemann in an article published in 1944 suggested the idea of stages of grief.[3] His study revealed the distinction between normal and abnormal grief reactions and the necessity of helping a bereaved person work through his grief so he could adjust better to life after his loss. The concept of stages of grief is not to imply that everyone must react in the same way or go through his grief experience in a clear stepping from one stage to the next, but it does denote the normal pattern to which most of us are subjected.

Shock. Our first reaction to the news of the death of someone close to us is shock. We simply cannot believe it. Shock is one of the natural ways our body reacts to provide us with a temporary escape from reality. At first we may be so stunned by the blow that we cannot do anything. We feel numb and anesthetized, bewildered and confused. Rossetti said that when his wife died his mind went completely blank. He learned nothing, saw nothing, and felt nothing. The only thing his passive mind could remember during this experience was that a certain flower had three petals. The shock of a great sorrow can be devastating. I have often heard people ask right after the loss, "What am I going to do? I can't live without him."

Bernadine Kreis observed in her helpful book *Up from Grief*, "Don't try to cope with shock. Let it be. Love does not accept death quickly," she continued. "It is not something which can be chopped down like a tree." [4] One day she recounted to a psychologist a recurring image of her husband which she continued to have, and she acknowledged that she simply could not understand its meaning.[5] On several occasions she saw the image of her husband standing inside the front door, and he always appeared as he did when he returned from work each day. As he smiled, she ran into his outstretched arms just as she had usually done and would lean against his chest. The psychologist informed her that the image had several meanings, not just one. "You could call it a shock-absorber," he said. "It was your way of alleviating your grief. Too, it was a normal reaction to the death of a beloved and vital figure in your life," he continued. "We don't stop loving someone at the precise instant he stops breathing. Your life was geared to his. Death came quickly, but the motion of your life together carried you forward on its own momentum as if he still lived." Shock, if it does not continue too long, can be an effective agent in assisting us in our initial grief reaction.

Distress, Suffering, or Agony. After the original shock, one moves into the second stage of grief which has many facets in it. It might be characterized as the suffering or distress stage. *Depression* is a normal feeling one often experiences in this stage soon after bereavement. A woman loses her husband; her loss is felt so keenly as the days go by that she wrestles with feelings of despondency and despair and does not know how she can face the empty house without him. A young daughter is killed in an automobile accident, and the parents stare at the wall with a sense of futility and loneliness. The grieving husband sits at his desk day after day, feeling fatigued, restless, unable to concentrate, anxious, and sensing a heavy fog weighted about his shoulders. Their names are Legion. Grief often plunges us into the "dark night of our soul," or into what John Bunyan called "the slough of despondency." The fog of depression can seem overwhelming, and it is difficult for us to realize that it is a normal reaction if it does not continue too long and that one day the clouds will lift and we will see the sun shining again.

One Sunday when I was in college I had the opportunity to preach in a small, rural church in a very mountainous section of Virginia. Early in the morning as I started to the church I encountered heavy patches of fog as I began the slow, steep climb up the mountainside. The further I went up the mountain, the worse the fog became. Several times I had to stop the car and get out to make sure I was still on the road. Slowly I made my way through the fog toward the top. A small flicker of light seemed to be searching for a pathway through the heavy layers of the fog. The whisk of light would dart in and out of the darkness as though it were playing a game of hide-and-seek with me. Suddenly as I reached the top of the mountain, brilliant sunshine flooded my car with its joyous radiance and drove away the darkness around me and within me.

The sunshine seemed to breathe a renewal of vitality and freshness to my spirit. It was then that the awareness hit me: The sun is always shining, even when the fog blocks it out; it may be hidden and not clearly visible at all times, but its existence need not be questioned. Most of the time we cannot see it in the fog, but the sun is still there. This became for me a parable about the presence of God. Though the fog of depression may sometimes crush us to our knees and make us feel unaware of his spirit, God is still there, just as the sun continues to shine behind the clouds with its warmth, power, and presence.

Abnormal Reactions. Grief usually obstructs our normal pattern of living. We are not sure where to turn or what to do sometimes, and these feelings create within us a sense of panic. One may wonder if he is losing his mind when this strange sense of lostness and isolation overtakes him. One may try hard to focus his attention on something else other than his grief, but no matter what one tries, his mind continues to return again and again to the loss one has experienced. We wonder if something is wrong with us. A grieving wife may stare out the window for an endless period of time, unaware of the dishes she is washing. After the recent loss of his wife, a husband may sit and look at an open letter without reading it at all as his mind wanders aimlessly. A person does not need to question his psychological soundness or his own sanity during this stage of grief. As long as one works through it, it may be a very normal reaction to an intensely personal grief experience.

No one can be expected to sever so quickly the tie which has bound one person's life to another. We have loved them too much to forget so quickly. As Rabbi Liebman in his chapter on "Grief's Slow Wisdom" reminds us, "the melody that the loved one played upon the piano of your life will never be played quite that way again, but we must not close the keyboard and allow the instrument to gather dust. We must seek out other artists of the spirit, new friends who gradually will help us to find the road to life again, who will walk that road with us." [6] Slowly the light of hope will break through the shaded windows of our spirit, and new possibilities and opportunities for renewed living will occur.

Guilt. The mixed bag of our emotions at the time of grief is difficult to understand or explain. Feelings of guilt will often arise

to haunt us and beckon us to the cellar of depression. "Oh, if
I had only got him to the hospital quicker, he would not have
died." "If the doctor had only come as soon as I called him."
"If I had not let Sally go riding with those boys, the accident
would never have happened." "Why didn't I realize she was as
sick as she said she was?" "I wish I could tell her again that
I'm sorry and that I really love her so much, but now she's gone
and I can never tell her." "Why did I fail him?"

Feelings of real and imagined guilt may fill our minds after
a loved one dies, things we might have done or not done, words
we wish we had said or could retract. Parents who lose a child
suffer strong guilt feelings because they feel that somehow as
a parent they may have failed the child or should have recognized
the need earlier, taken more care, provided greater supervision,
recognized symptoms earlier, or other attitudes. Whether it comes
from the sudden loss of a husband with a heart attack, a wife
to cancer, a parent to a lengthy illness, or a child with a dread
disease, feelings of guilt may arise as a normal part of the burden
of stress from one's bereavement. Thoughts of old arguments, hurt
feelings, repressed feelings, or delayed actions may also increase
guilt feelings. The more sensitive a person is, the depth of his
love for the deceased, the greater his awareness of the tie that
has been severed by his acute loss, the stronger may be his inner
turmoil of conflict. Kierkegaard once noted, "The greater the
genius, the more profoundly he discovers guilt." [7]

Guilt and self-condemnation are universal expressions of a normal process of emotional response to grief, but prolonged periods
of melancholia or depression may indicate an unwillingness on
the part of the griever to deal with his own conflicting feelings.
Many times these feelings may need to be verbalized to a close
friend or minister before one can resolve them.

Hostility. Grief usually arouses feelings of anger within us. We
may feel angry at the doctor, nurse, minister, funeral director,
a friend, or anyone who happens to cross our mind when the
reality of what has happened to us begins to dawn. Kreis and
Pattie observed within themselves, "Grief's anger is irrational,

born of frustration, and often acted out in a curious kind of rebellion." [8] We want to strike out at someone because of the deep hurt and the sinking feeling we have within us.

Our displaced anger may often be directed against our loved one for leaving us alone or for not preparing us better. Sometimes our hostility is even raised against God; we have a feeling that he has let us down by allowing this death to occur. "Why did God let it happen? Why, oh, why?" we often ask. We are so afraid of expressing our feelings. When small children suffer pain, loss, or hurt, they do not attempt to camouflage or disguise their feelings but cry, yell, and express them openly. In times of grief it might be healthier for us if we could learn to be more childlike in our willingness to be open about our feelings and express them instead of pushing them deep down within us.

Destructive Reactions to Grief Experiences

Considering the disruptive force which grief hurls into our lives, it is impossible not to respond to such a severe rupture in one's usual pattern of daily living. We will react to its schism in a way which eventually will be destructive or constructive to our own stability as a person. But we will react! It appears much wiser to look at grief before one is thrust into its flooding stream and its undertow has swept away much of our sense of clear perspective. Notice first some destructive responses to grief.

Overactivity. Someone has observed that "grief thrives in the soil of idleness." Without question, this is true; bereavement can be eased some by keeping busy. Fortunately for us there is work which must be done, duties which press in upon us to be performed, necessities which demand attention. These keep us from losing touch with many practical things which simply have to be taken care of.

Although work may often serve as a legitimate anodyne for grief, on the other hand, busyness may also become a means of denying grief. A husband who has lost his wife can throw himself into his work in an effort to blot out the reality of her death. A mother who is bereaved at the death of a child will sometimes become enamored with club, community, school, or church activities to such an excessive degree that she loses sight of the rest of her family and their needs. All of this activity is really a cover up to keep from facing and dealing with her personal loss. Work is often a therapeutic outlet for grief, but when our efforts become a means of evading our loss, then busyness has become a destructive factor instead of a healthy stimulus to reconstructing our lives.

Denial. The sudden shock of grief may cause us to push the fact of our loss from our mind. We are not willing to accept it or come to grips with what has really taken place, and so we may cover up our real feelings with a pretense of outward poise and apparent, courageous adjustment. *The Buffalo Evening News* carried the story of a woman, now in a state hospital, who is an extreme example of death denial. The body of her mother was preserved between mattresses for fifteen years by various potions and oils. This almost perfectly preserved mummy, Charles Bachmann observes, illustrates the great lengths to which some people may go to avert the reality of loss.⁹

This may be an extreme and bizarre example, nevertheless, we all know of families who have turned a room of a loved one into a kind of shrine. Everything must remain just as Jimmy left it—no picture can be moved; no toy can be given away; the clothes remain in the drawers and the closet. The room gives evidence that the parents are still awaiting the child's return and, therefore, is an obvious denial of the reality of his death.

Often I have heard people express a sort of denial when they stated: "I can't believe he is really gone. I feel he is still here with me in the house." "I keep her clothes ready for her, feeling she may come back any moment to wear them." "I come downstairs and fix breakfast and wonder if he is not really just asleep upstairs." "I keep telling myself that he is just away on another business trip and will come walking in the front door any day now." Grief cannot be denied or postponed indefinitely without dangerous consequences. Facing it is inevitable.

Delay. Delay is another form of denial; it simply attempts to postpone or push into the unconscious mind any grief response.

Delay or repression of grief often results in many emotional or physical ailments. No one can expect to ignore or escape feelings of acute loss by burying them deep inside himself. Anger, depression, resentment, fear, guilt, and many other forces will find avenues of expressing themselves if grief is consciously or unconsciously repressed.

Withdrawal. In the face of grief the overpowering urge is the impulse to run away from it, withdraw into ourselves, or flee and escape its reality. We feel like the psalmist who said: "O that I had wings like a dove! I would fly away and be at rest." So we run away into our work, our clubs, or church. We escape to the seashore, mountain lodge, or desert inn. We rush into ceaseless conversation about the weather, clothes, the house, friends. We flee into a book, a hobby, the television, sewing, cooking, eating, drugs, or drinking.

The Swiss physician Paul Tournier has written a chapter in his book *The Healing of Persons* [10] entitled "Flight," which is the way many seek to escape their problems in life. In this chapter he depicts man's flight into dreams as man attempts to escape a painful reality by turning to fantasy. The flight into the past is a means of avoiding present problems by focusing one's attention on what has been; the flight into the future provides a way to escape the imperfections of the present by projecting indistinct plans about tomorrow. The flight into disease offers to us a means of escaping some difficult responsibility or a way of focusing attention upon ourselves by becoming ill. The flight into work furnishes an escape from sad or bitter situations, whereas the flight into religion itself may serve as an effort to sever one's responsibility for the problems of the world.

Withdrawal can take many forms as a person seeks various means of avoiding and fleeing from his loss. Some choose alcohol, drugs, sex tangles, or even suicide. I can still hear him now: "I do not want to live," he said. "Sometimes it is easier to face death than to face life." Burdens seem so heavy that some few see the only solution in an absolute attempt to escape life, and so they commit suicide—the final and complete act of withdrawal.

Self-pity. How easy it is for someone who is bereaved to fall into the attitude of self-pity and focus all of his attention on how tragic and awful everything really is for him. He muses over his grief and cries, "Unfair, unfair. Why would God allow this to happen to me?" he asks, "It's just so unfair!"

Self-pity crashes our emotions with a disintegrating blow and shatters any reasonable sense of balance and perspective. So we refuse invitations to be with people or to eat a meal with a friend. We remain alone at home and flounder in self-pity without allowing anyone even to give us a hand to help lift us out of the depths of our grief. "Why has this happened to me?" we cry. "Why not somebody else? Why not that old incorrigible drunk who is seen every day?—Why does he live to be eighty? Why didn't God take him instead of my bright, brilliant child—or my husband who had so much to offer?" A solution is difficult to reach, however, as long as we are controlled by the emotion which refuses to view life from any other perspective than through the dark glasses of self-pity.

Constructive Responses to Grief

Although our grief reactions are seldom logical, it seems appropriate to try to examine some responses which may prove helpful in the time of bereavement. Every grieving person wants to be able to face the past, present, and future again. He longs to pick up life's fragments and make sense again of them. He yearns to put aside his mourning clothes and rise up again and see the glory of a sunrise, smell the beauty of a rose, and feel the radiance of a smile as he picks up the pieces of his life and begins to rebuild it. Bereavement, if not handled correctly, can develop into a morbid grief which can cut one off from himself and others and make him feel like he is cut off even from God. The work of normal grief has been called "the illness that heals itself," whereas excessive grief has been seen as "the enemy of the living." The following steps are offered as suggested guidelines for facing grief constructively.

Accept Your Grief. In an article entitled "Do Christians Believe in Death?" Burton H. Throckmorton, Jr., has noted that most Christians seem unable to come to terms with death and continue to deny its reality and cling to many primitive ideas about it. His study concludes with the observation: "The gospel does not hold that there is no death. The Good News is that there is ground for hope in life out of death. Out of death." [11] Much of our attention is directed to death-denying attitudes and practices. But a healthy response to death is to see it and accept it as a real part of every human life, to realize that no one escapes it ultimately.

C. S. Lewis stated that it was hard for him to have patience with people who say: " 'There is no death' or 'Death doesn't matter.' There is death. And whatever is matters, and whatever happens has consequences, and it and they are irrevocable and irreversible. You might as well say that birth doesn't matter. Is anything more certain," he asked, "than that in all those vast times and spaces, if I were allowed to search them, I should nowhere find her face, her voice, her touch? She died. She is dead. Is the word so difficult to learn?" [12]

Even as Christians we must acknowledge the reality of death. This does not mean that we welcome it or can explain it, but it is an awareness that death touches the life of all—strangers down the street or around the world, neighbors next door, friends across the country, relatives within our own house or nearby. Here is the way Edna St. Vincent Millay expressed it:

> Down, down, down into the darkness of the grave,
> Gently they go, the beautiful, the tender, the kind;
> Quietly they go, the intelligent, the witty, the brave,
> I know. But I do not approve. And I am not resigned.[13]

Who does not grieve over the loss of someone? Although the Christian should not accept his loss fatalistically or simply as something which God has deliberately willed or sent as a punishment for his or someone else's sins, he does seek to affirm his own sorrow with the spirit of Jeremiah, "This is my grief, and I must bear it" (Jer. 10:19, KJV). Even in the midst of his tears, he affirms death as a part of life and declares with Job: "The Lord gave, and the Lord has taken away; blessed be the name of the Lord" (Job 1:21).

I was with a woman in the hospital corridor when she received news of her husband's death. At first she did not say a word but just buried her head on my shoulder and sobbed. In a few moments she turned to the doctor and said: "Thank you, Doctor, I know you did everything you could, but he just had too much against him this time." Through moist eyes she listened as the doctor described what he and others had attempted to do to save her husband's life from his second massive heart attack. After the doctor departed she wept again for awhile and then asked, "What must I do now?" What she did was to go home and slowly began to work through her sorrow—first by accepting it and not denying her normal feelings engendered by it. Counselors have observed that it usually takes from three to six months to accept fully the idea of the loss of a loved one, but this is only a general pattern and not necessarily an exact time scale for all people. The first step toward healing in bereavement is the acceptance of the death of a loved one.

Reflect on Your Grief. You will do this without the urging of anyone. Many will offer bad advice by suggesting that we should "not think about our loss"; we should put our sorrow "out of our mind"; "don't even let yourself think about what has really happened." Don't listen to those who tell you to put your grief out of your mind because you cannot. You must learn to live with it and the memories with which it floods your mind. Kreis and Pattie have advised, "Every death leaves its scars on the griever and part of a healthy recovery is in remembering." [14]

You will aways be haunted by memories, and as quickly as you can learn to face them the better your adjustment will be. You will need to look at pictures from the past; listen to familiar music you both loved; walk down familiar paths and visit beloved shops; look at favorite chairs, or toys, or books, or clothes; talk with friends with whom the deceased was close. Live with the memories; don't run from them. Learn to live with them until you can express thanks for the gift of the life with whom you had occasion to share a portion of time. Learn to rejoice in the collective memories which this shared life has deposited in your mental reservoir.

Recovering from grief never means a total erasure of all memories of the deceased. This cannot be done nor should it be done. The deceased was a unique person who touched your life in a special way, and no one else can take his place and affect you in quite the same way as he did. Anyone else who may enter your life will not take the deceased person's place but will assume his own special place.

You will also reflect on the reason you are now in your sorrow. You will want to know what caused the death of your loved one, the type of illness or disease, whether anything could have been done to prevent it, and if anyone was responsible? All kinds of questions may arise in your grief. Face them honestly and openly; answer the ones you can; seek guidance from others; remember that many of our "whys" simply have no pat answers, no clear, known solution; and look for the possible way that even our sorrow can be used for ultimate good. This latter is probably asking too much, in the early stages, but sometimes in retrospect we can discover lessons even in our deepest sorrows and darkest valleys.

Express Your Grief. Crying is a normal, healthy emotional outlet for any person suffering from a grief experience. Unfortunately our society has tried to suppress this common reaction by saying: "Don't break down now, you know he wouldn't want that." "Don't cry any more, that won't bring your mother back." "Come on son, be a man now, don't cry." The deep ache, sore hurt, and bottled-up feelings need to be expressed, and no mourner need feel any sense of apology or disgrace for weeping. Do so unashamedly—in the privacy of your room, on the shoulder of a relative or friend—wherever there are understanding friends. Feel free to express your grief. The Chinese have an old proverb, "If you do not weep outwardly, you will weep inwardly."

Recently I heard a funeral director share a healthy philosophy about their funeral home: "The funeral home is a place where

we feel comfortable around people who cry in times of sorrow."
Your minister and others who are aware of their benefit will
welcome your tears, because they know that crying is a part of
the therapeutic process of healing. Jesus himself wept beside the
grave of his friend Lazarus, and the Bible directs us "to weep
with those who weep." Edgar N. Jackson has reminded us that
it is important to be aware of the function of tears. "It serves
little purpose to try to prevent the use of nature's own safety
valves." " 'The consoling effect of quiet tears,' " he continues,
quoting Gert Heilbrunn, " 'suggests an influence as comforting
and soothing as the soft flow of the tears.' " [15]

Unexpressed grief may only complicate a person's life. The
failure for friends to allow the mourner to express his grief could
force him to disguise and suppress his real emotions. Kreis and
Pattie bring this out vividly in their account of a young divorcee
who lost her little girl and later committed suicide herself.[16] In
a note she wrote:

"This is the tenth night, I've sat in this empty room holding this
little bottle of sleeping pills. Why don't I swallow them, why do I wait?
Why do I write all this down? Because I want to talk—I need to talk.
I wish I felt bitter like I did when Jim and I were divorced. Then
it was just anger and disappointment. Yes, that's how it was then.
Whatever the pain of it I didn't expect it to last. That's the important
part. I could cry then, I can't cry now. When Penny died everyone
said: 'You are taking it so well. You're wonderful! So brave!' Isn't that
a laugh? Complimenting me for being a Zombie!"

Express your grief outwardly.

Share Your Grief. With the pain of grief comes the need to
talk about your loss. The woman who committed suicide might
not have taken her life if she could have found someone to listen.
Share your grief with someone you trust, someone with whom
you feel you can reveal your inner feelings. Talking about the
deceased helps the bereaved person to face the reality of death.
In bereavement you will find that you want to talk about the
last moments or days of his life; to reflect on events and ac-

complishments in his life; to speak of joys and sorrows, dreams, and disappointments; or to idealize the deceased. The exteriorizing of your inner feelings about your loss will help you to confront your conflicting emotions of love and hate, guilt and peace, sorrow and release, sadness and relief, depression and hope, and many others. Shakespeare's Macbeth expressed it realistically:

> Give sorrow words; the grief that does not speak,
> Whispers the o'er-fraught heart, and bids it break.

You will soon find that you should not and cannot share your grief with everybody. Many do not want to hear it—it frightens them; others do not want to take the time; some will change the subject quickly, hoping to get your mind off "morbid things"; some others want you to listen to their problems; a few will listen and care. Find these and share your grief with them; they want to help you bear it. It may be a friend, a relative, or your minister.

Even after three years a woman was still not able to adjust to the death of her husband.[17] All of his personal things were still kept in the home just as they had been before his death. When she found that she was going to have to move to another residence, she called her pastor to share a strange dream she had. In her dream she was packing to go to the new house, but her husband refused to go. She tried to use physical strength to force him to go, but he resisted. Finally, she said, she pulled so hard that she pulled him apart and packed the pieces in a suitcase, but when she arrived at the new house she opened the suitcase and to her surprise found it empty.

In response to the pastor's inquiry of what the dream meant to her, she stated, through her tears, that she had been struggling to decide what she should do with her dead husband's belongings. Now she felt she would not keep them any longer. The next day she called to tell her pastor that she had disposed of all her husband's things and was moving into her new home to make a fresh beginning. The dream and someone who would listen enabled her to verbalize her feelings and find release.

Direct Your Grief. Grief can become a destructive force in our lives if all of our attention is focused only on our own loss and sorrow. We can spend all of our energy and efforts drowning in self-pity, or we can direct our sorrow toward some meaningful end. Only those who have known genuine sorrow are able to lift others who fall under the weight of sorrow's burden. When you have seen the "light at the end of the tunnel," then you can guide others who walk through the dark valley of grief toward the light.

John Gunther, author of such famous books as *Inside Europe* and *Inside U.S.A.*, wrote a small volume over twenty years ago which was his memoir of his son's battle to defy a dread disease. At seventeen years of age his young son died of a brain tumor. Mr. Gunther's small book is one man's attempt to direct his grief to assist others to face death with more courage, confidence, and hope as they reflect on his young son's battle and defiance over death's sting. *Death Be Not Proud* has helped thousands to face and accept death and grief from a little different perspective because one man chose to direct his grief.

When the famous American actress Helen Hayes suffered the death of her daughter, she declared: "Before, I had been concerned primarily with myself and my family, unaware in the human spirit of the need of people for one another. But now I knew that I, too, had to be a living part of God's world of people." Those who have suffered much are able to help others in their time of grief. The apostle Paul has reminded us, "Bear one another's burdens, and so fulfil the law of Christ" (Gal. 6:2).

Surrender Your Grief to God

When grief comes to us we feel that it is uniquely our own. So it is, but grief comes to all. The distinctive Christian insight is that we do not have to face it alone—we have the Presence of Another—the very source of life itself. As Christians, we seek to stand in the storm of life aware of deeper resources we have available to uphold our sagging spirits. Although the Christian faith does not offer us a "protection plan" against all problems and difficulties, or a "safety zone" insulating us from all the bumps, bruises, and tragedies, or an "immunization program" against all diseases and sufferings, it does provide us with an inner security which is based on the abiding strength of God's presence. "Who shall separate us from the love of Christ?" cries the apostle Paul.

Shall tribulation, or distress, or persecution, or famine, or nakedness, or peril, or sword? No, in all these things we are more than conquerors through him who loved us. For I am sure that neither death, nor life, nor angels, nor principalities, nor things present, nor things to come, nor powers, nor height, nor depth, nor anything else in all creation, will be able to separate us from the love of God in Christ Jesus our Lord (Rom. 8:35, 37-39).

The word *comfort* in our contemporary vocabulary has become symbolic of a soft, sweet, smooth kind of devotion, like the tender care of a mother for her baby. But this was not so with the original meaning of the word. The word *comfort* is derived from two words *com*, "with" plus *fortis*, "strength." When Isaiah declares, "Comfort ye, my people," he is crying, "Strengthen ye, my people." The comfort which comes from the abiding Presence of God is an inner strength which fortifies us to face any situation because we are aware that we do not confront it isolated and alone.

Marc Connally's play *Green Pastures* closes with the crucifixion of Jesus. The angels in heaven can hear the human cries which rise from the earth. Seeing Jesus with the load of the cross on his back they declare: "Look at that man carrying his cross up the hill! That's a terrible burden for one man to carry!" Indeed it was. But because he shared our life, struggled with our problems, bore our problems, sustained our infirmities, we know that we can cast our burdens on him because he understands and cares. Because he identified with mankind in life and death, we are able to listen, understand, and respond to the words of Jesus when he said: "Come to me, all who labor and are heavy laden, and I will give you rest. Take my yoke upon you, and learn from me; for I am gentle and lowly in heart, and you will find rest for your souls. For my yoke is easy, and my burden is light"

(Matt. 11:28-30).

The National Gallery in Washington, D. C., at one time displayed a picture of the crucified Christ which was captivating to the viewer. When you first look at the painting, you see only Christ hanging on the cross, isolated and alone, surrounded by dense darkness. Suddenly as you continue to gaze at the picture, another presence seems to peer out of the background—and you are aware that it is the very presence of God himself whose face is filled with sorrow, whose agony seems more intense. One can almost hear the apostle Paul shouting from within the painting: "God was in Christ reconciling the world to himself" (2 Cor. 5:19, NEB).

We know then that God does share our sorrow and understands it. Just as any parent seeks to embrace his own children with love and understanding in times of sadness, defeat, or sorrow, even more so are we aware of God's desire to support and share our grief with us. The God who continues age after age to bear the burdens, sorrows, sins, and sufferings of mankind can surely carry one more ache and sustain you and me with a deeper fellowship of his spirit. Surrender your grief to God with the assurance that the Good Shepherd will undergird you and place his strong shoulder under the yoke of your burden and enable you to endure it. At the death of her brother, Jesus asked Martha if she believed he was the resurrection and the life. She replied, "Yes, Lord, I believe." We will never meet grief victoriously until we are able to trust in the power and love of God.

3
Helping a Friend in Grief

Grief is one of the most exacting, difficult, and final of all our emotional reactions in life. To face grief is difficult but to face it alone is even worse. We live as though death does not exist for us or our immediate family. We acknowledge that other people will one day die, but we live out our existence as though death will never happen to us or our loved ones. Our society constantly attempts to push the reality of death out of our minds. We do not want to hear about it; we disguise it, run from it, or ignore it. Most of our life is lived in an attitude of pretense regarding death.

A classic illustration of the way the mind sometimes operates to reject the idea of death is vividly delineated in the film *An Occurrence at Owl Creek Bridge.*[1] This film won the Grand Prize in 1962 at the Cannes Festival and an Academy Award in 1964 as the best live-action, short-subject. A young, wealthy plantation owner was captured by Federal soldiers in Alabama during the Civil War. The soldiers quickly formed an execution party to hang this Southern civilian who had assisted the enemy. As the young planter stands on the narrow plank, with a hemp rope around his neck and his hands tied behind his back, he gazes into the swirling water racing madly beneath the crossties of the Owl Creek Bridge and ponders an escape plan.

Suddenly he feels the rope break as he crashes into the water and then he struggles beneath the surface to set his hands and feet free. With lungs almost bursting, he makes it to the surface to elude the soldier's bullets as he swims with the current away from the bridge. When he reaches the shore, he runs, it seems, mile after mile to escape the soldiers. Finally he reaches his plantation and falls forward to embrace his wife who is standing, smiling, with open arms. At that very moment in the film, however, the scene changes abruptly back to the bridge and the viewer is shaken by the sight of the grotesque, dead figure of the young civilian, swinging gently from side to side, as he hangs beneath the timbers of the Owl Creek Bridge. The message of the film seems to be saying that man strives to deceive himself that he can escape death but ultimately the reality confronts us as we reach the end of our rope.

We live with this attitude of death denial, unwilling to acknowledge that death is real, but sometimes it stabs us awake so that we cannot ignore it—when death takes someone we love—a child, a husband, a wife, a mother, a father, or a friend. Then the bruise of grief seems to blacken our spirits, our attitude, our perspective, our body, our mind, our emotions—our very existence. In this time of darkness often a friend can help to bring some light by his presence, concern, and sympathy. Fewer crises in life afford friends the opportunity for genuine ministry as does grief. Shakespeare expressed that thought this way:

> Wherever sorrow is, relief would be:
> If you do sorrow at my grief in love,
> By giving love, your sorrow and my grief
> Were both extermin'd.[2]

Unsatisfactory Ways of Offering Help

Even our best intention may sometimes fall far short of our genuine desire to be of some assistance to another in times of grief. Greater good, however, could probably be done if we learned some things to avoid as we approach our friends in their bereavement. Here are some suggestions to enable you to shun some bad advice which, sometimes, all of us may feel inclined to offer.

Don't put the load of the world on the griever. A quick response of many to one who is bereaved is to remind him of how bad off many others may be. "Yes," someone may state, "I know it's bad to lose a child, but do you realize that Mrs. Jones lost three children in an accident last year." Another may thoughtlessly declare, "I know your loss seems heavy, but think of the thousands of homes where grief struck when the earthquake hit." "I know you must be having a hard time accepting Jack's death," another friend admonishes, "but remember how many homes felt sorrow when the French overseas jet crashed killing the one hundred twenty-one Atlanta citizens who were aboard." "I know your mother lingered a long time from her stroke, but I have a friend who had to take care of her ill mother as a bed patient for fifteen years." Others say: "Just accept it; it's God's will, you know."

Several years ago a devastating landslide and flood occurred after weeks of rain had saturated the mountainside in Nelson County, Virginia. Without warning in the middle of the night, part of the mountainside just slid down the hill, and the rivers were so swollen that the banks could not contain the raging force of the waters which rushed down the mountain, crushing, twisting, destroying, mutilating anything or anyone that got in its angry pathway. Hundreds of homes lost family members and whole families were swept away; everyone in the county felt the sting of death and grief.

After the ravaging night had passed, the people were shaken and appalled by the extent of the devastation which had unfolded in one short night. Few could take in what had happened so quickly, much less believe or understand it. I sat in a small, crowded, rural church with a fellow minister and looked into the faces of the three children of my brother-in-law's sister's family who had survived the flood. These children had lost their parents and three other brothers and sisters.

That day and since, little was said about the number alone of anyone's loss; everyone felt the sorrow of another and suffered and ached with him. The knowledge of how comprehensive the damage had been and how extensive the grief was did not ease the burden which everyone bore, it only served to heighten the sorrow. No one received much comfort from the comment, "Be thankful you still have one child or two or three." A person's grief is real, and placing the sadness of the world on his shoulders in the time of his bereavement does not aid him. It only enhances his awareness of the magnitude of suffering and grief.

Don't encourage isolation. Grief is not the time to direct a person on some personal period of soul-searching and introspection. The griever will do enough of that on his own anyway. Several years ago Simon and Garfunkel wrote a song entitled "I Am a Rock." In it is reflected the spirit of one who seeks to avoid life, isolated and hidden from its cares and responsibilities.

This philosophy is totally unreal. No man can be like a rock and remain untouched by those around him. Absolute isolation is a myth; we must live in a community and in cooperation and contact with other people. The problems of pollution, war, and disease; the necessity of insurance, police protection, highway safety laws, and medical attention; the dependence on others for the production and distribution of food, milk, clothing, and other essentials are only a few of the many areas which depict our mutual connection and involvement with the lives of others.

This mutual interdependence was hammered home rather strongly in my mind by an old story which happened before organs were equipped with electronic power and had to be hand pumped in order to produce the sound. One night a famous concert organist was giving a recital. While he played, a young fellow, hidden behind a screen, pumped with all the strength he had. During the intermission the organist was standing in the wings and the little boy came up to him and declared: "Aren't we great!" Rather sharply the organist retorted, "What do you mean, 'We'?" After the intermission, the organist sat down again at the keyboard and pressed down on the keys and not a sound came. He pressed again, still not a sound. Then the young lad poked his head around the screen and asked, "Now, who's we?" Who are we indeed!

No man can live separated from his fellowman. He needs strength, companionship, love, support, and encouragement from others. To be isolated and alone in one's bereavement is one of the worst torments any person might have to endure. It is true that every grief experience is a lonely, personal journey which no one else can take for you. There is an aloneness which no one else can bear for you; there is a stabbing isolation which cannot be communicated; there is an empty feeling which no words can fill; there is an ache which no one else can ever touch.

Every grief carries with it a distinctive loneliness. This loneliness makes the burden difficult to carry. Our friends can never fully lift this sense of aloneness from us, but without their interest and concern it would be even more difficult to bear. The thought that no one cared could be the most devastating blow of all. Isolation will only encourage self-pity and withdrawal which may propel the griever deeper into the far country of loneliness and make it more difficult for him to find the way back. "The sting of death is solitude," states Paul Ramsey. "Desertion is more choking than death and more feared."

Don't support an activity syndrome. Words rush to our lips before we realize what we are encouraging when we say to the grief sufferer: "Try to put Tom's death out of your mind and find something that needs to be done around the house." "Get back to work as quickly as you can and you will gradually forget as you get busy again." "Take up a new hobby—golf or fishing might help you to forget." "Now, Susan, what you really need is a long vacation—go see some new places, travel a lot—this will help you put Larry's death out of your mind."

All of these suggestions direct the griever simply to get busy doing something, and this busyness will make him forget his sorrow. Work, travel, hobbies—all may help some and be therapeutic, to a degree, but they are anodynes and not permanent solutions to the problem of grief. Grief must be confronted to be resolved; pushing it deep within one's self or losing one's self in work, recreation, civic or church organizations will not remove the bereavement until it has first been faced. Once grief has been met and its reality accepted and dealt with, then one's activity can take on a more meaningful and helpful function in a person's life.

Don't minimize another person's grief. Interestingly enough no one ever views his own grief as insignificant. We often have a tendency, nevertheless, to depreciate someone else's loss. "Don't

cry," I've heard people say. "You will get over it. Time will heal."
"I know it seems bad to you now, but think how much worse
it could have been if he had lingered like poor old . . ." In a
sense what this approach offers us is a form of death denial. It
acknowledges that death has transpired, but it also asserts that
our grief could not be nearly as bad with our loved one or friend
as it was with someone else. Granger E. Westberg has observed,
"We grieve over the loss of anything important."

Grief takes many shapes and directions. Grief may result from
many things: the loss of a job; the loss of physical senses, such
as sight or hearing; the loss of a home through a natural disaster
or financial setback. A move to a new city or going away to
college or military service may cause grief. A favorite pet dies;
the children grow up, get married, and move away; recognition
does not come in your job or community; your health breaks;
you retire; your marriage fails and you get a divorce; your son
or daughter gets in trouble or turns to drugs—or one of a thousand
other things may happen to produce grief. All of these are in
addition to the death of someone close to you. No matter how
small your grief may appear to someone else, to you it is real
and vitally important. To ridicule it or to disparage it will only
deepen intense feelings of rejection.

Recently I spoke with a woman who expressed deep feelings
of grief over the loss of a horse. For thirty-two years this animal
had been a vital part of her life. She had ridden him faithfully
for sixteen years until the animal's health no longer permitted
it and, then, for the remainder of the years the horse became
a dear pet she loved and cared for. At his death she felt genuine
sadness and bereavement.

I recall the intense feelings of separation and loneliness which
I experienced as a child when I lost various pets. But even before
the loss of pets, I recall the strange stirrings within as I discovered
a dead bird in the grass and raised the question, "What's wrong
with this bird, Mother?" "It's dead," she replied. "What does
dead mean?" I asked. The answer does not penetrate a child's
mind fully but an impression is made; a new note is sounded;

a forbidden door is opened; an awesome reality is disclosed; a new lesson is learned. To a child these "griefs" are real and should not be "put down." The helpful facing of these smaller griefs can enable a child to meet the larger "griefs" more constructively later in his life.

Edgar N. Jackson has written an understanding and helpful book *Telling a Child About Death* which parents will find very useful. Most children have their first encounter with death through the loss of a pet. Instead of minimizing this loss, it affords a real opportunity to talk about death and help the child begin his slow acquaintance with it. Whether a person is young or old, whether his grief is over the loss of something seemingly small or great, his personal grief should be taken seriously and treated wisely to guide him to a deeper insight into the reality and value of both life and death.

Don't offer to the bereaved a view of life seen only through rose-colored glasses. Help them face the awful reality of sin and evil which exist in our world. Don't ignore it or pretend it doesn't exist. Help them sense death and grief as a part of the fabric of life. We noted earlier that grief often results in shock, depression, anxiety, hostility, frustration, and other physical, psychological, and emotional responses. Unfortunately some people leave the impression with the griever that all will be well—"God will take care of you; you have nothing to be afraid of." Some want to project an optimism which is unrealistic.

Lucy in Charles Schulz's *Peanuts* voices this kind of outlook on life. "Sometimes I get discouraged," says Lucy. "Well, Lucy," Charlie Brown states, "Life does have its ups and downs, you know." Forcefully Lucy asserts: "But why? Why should it?! Why can't my life be all 'ups'? If I want all 'ups,' why can't I have them? Why can't I just move from one 'up' to another 'up'? Why can't I just go from an 'up' to an 'upper-up'? I don't want any 'downs!' I just want 'ups' and 'ups' and 'ups!' " Standing off to the side, Charlie Brown declares for us all, "I can't stand it." [3]

None of us can stand an unrealistic view of life which fails to take into account the valleys as well as the mountaintops, the

thorns with the roses, the low as well as the high, the night as
well as the day, the rain as well as the sunshine, the bad as well
as the good. All sunshine makes a desert according to an old
Arab proverb. Our lives are not filled with all bright spots; low
moments of disappointment, failure, sorrow, grief, and even death
cross the life of us all.

The Christian affirms that God does not protect him from all
problems or sorrows but that God is present in the low moments
as well as the high. "Night brings out stars," Gamaliel Bailey
declares, "as sorrow shows us truths." The true measure of a man
is his response to failure or sickness, grief or suffering, and his
unwillingness to be defeated by defeat, crushed by failure, broken
by illness, frustrated by discomfort, baffled by disappointment,
or conquered by death.

The roll call of the ages points to chapters forged in time by:
Joseph in Egypt, Moses in the Wilderness, Elijah on Mt. Carmel,
the disciple Peter in the courtyard of denial, Jesus on the cross,
Paul in prison. The roll call continues in modern times: John
Bunyan's twelve years in a Bedford jail, Milton's blindness, Beetho-
ven's deafness, Dostoevsky's epilepsy, Victor Hugo's exile, Phillips
Brooks' failure as a teacher, Alexander Pope's deformed appearance, Abraham Lincoln's political defeats, Harry S Truman's
humble background, Einstein's lack of formal education, Helen
Keller's blindness and deafness, Martin Luther King's black skin—
the list could continue on and on. Their chapters are written
within history. They used defeat, failure, limitations, or suffering
and rose above them, or through them, or because of them to
richer contributions to the world and deeper personal growth.

In his book *Why Do Men Suffer?* Leslie Weatherhead has
written a moving tribute to his mother and sister in his dedication
of the book to them in their struggle against suffering. The dedication reads:

DEDICATED
In unfading remembrance
to
Elizabeth Mary Weatherhead

my Mother,
and to
Muriel Weatherhead
my Sister,
whose bodies were defeated in the battle against painful
disease; but who, from that defeat, wrested a spiritual
victory which challenged and inspired all who knew them,
and made glad the heart of God. And to all proud
sufferers who, with broken body and unbroken spirit, are
seeking to achieve for themselves and for others
The Conquest of Suffering [4]

"Man is so great that his greatness appears even in his consciousness of misery," says Pascal the French philosopher. "A tree does not know itself to be miserable. It is true that it is misery indeed to know one's self to be miserable; but then it is greatness also. In this way all man's miseries go to prove his greatness. They are the miseries of a mighty potentate, of a dethroned monarch." Pascal concludes: "Notwithstanding the sight of all the miseries which wring us and threaten our destruction, we have still an instinct that we cannot repress, which elevates us above our sorrow."

Ways of Helping the Bereaved

It is often easy to speak of the things we should not do; we turn now to some brief suggestions of ways we might help someone in time of grief. These suggestions are practices which either those in grief experiences found to be helpful to them, or which I have found to be a helpful means of strengthening a friend during the crisis of bereavement.

Make yourself available to the one who is bereaved. Be there! When you learn that a friend has had a death in the family, go and be with him. Don't ask the bereaved person if there is something you can do; either ask another relative or simply look around and see what needs to be done. Someone must answer the telephone; someone needs to greet friends at the door; someone needs to care for small children if there are any; someone may need to do some washing, ironing, or cooking. A bereaved person does not need instant sermons, quotations of long Scripture passages, or a philosophy of life. What he needs is you—your personal presence means more than calls, cards, telegrams, or anything else. Tournier has reminded us: "He who loves understands, and he who understands loves. One who feels understood feels loved and one who feels loved feels sure of being understood." [5]

Be present and be willing to touch grieving friends—they need to feel the support of your hand, the assurance of your embrace, the strength of your arm, the sympathy of your kiss, the concern of your tears. The greatest gift you can share with them is yourself—it's the only real extension of your personhood. Ashly Montagu has called "touch" the mother of all the senses.[6] The aspiration to cultivate the human touch is to desire the compassion of the Christ who was willing to reach out and touch, even the untouchable—the leper, the outcast, sinners, the sick, the dying, the beggar, a small child, a government official in need, or a theologian who sought him out by night. His touch embraced all.

Richard Baxter, who was criticized by his friends for grieving too long over the death of his wife, declared, "I will not be judged by those who have never known the like." Those who have felt the pangs of sorrow can reach out a sympathetic hand of understanding because they have felt as their friends have felt; they have ached; they have cried; they have walked the dark valley of grief before, and now they can extend a hand.

H. H. Rowley described the Christian as one who is much more than a postman who drops a letter in the box and leaves without any sense of obligation or responsibility for the outcome. God seeks to use his children as his agents of reconciliation in the world. Luther said that each Christian is to be a "little Christ," an extension of Christ himself into the world. Life is not meant to be lived as a solo but as a chorus and the Christian cannot evade the biblical injunctions: "Bear ye one another's burdens and so fulfil the law of Christ" (Gal. 6:2). "We then that are strong shall bear the infirmities of the weak" (Rom. 15:1, KJV).

The words of Jesus echo in our minds, "Inasmuch as ye have done it unto one of the least . . . ye have done it unto me" (Matt. 25:40, KJV).

Some churches have a helpful practice called a "sharing ministry." The general idea behind this ministry is that someone in the church who has had a similar grief experience or a parallel problem with the present sufferer will be notified, and he in turn seeks to assist the griever through his difficult time. For example, if a young couple experiences the death of a small child, a couple in the church who has had this same loss and found peace with themselves, life, and God can minister to this couple in the name and spirit of an understanding Christ.

Arthur Pearson was one of the best-loved Englishmen of his time. His eyes had been weak from birth, and his life had been a race with blindness. At the age of forty-seven he was told he would lose his vision within a year. In 1913 he became permanently blind. Less than six months later, World War I broke out and blind soldiers were brought back from the front lines to hospitals near London. One young soldier, on hearing the news that he had lost his sight, went into hysterics. It was then that the hospital sent for Pearson, hoping that another man who had lost his vision might help this young soldier back to the road of recovery to begin his life anew.

This encounter with a blind soldier opened up for Pearson a whole new life's work. He organized a hospital for blind soldiers, and by the end of the war he had worked with seventeen hundred blind men at St. Dunston's. The blind soldiers responded to the helping hand of the man who sought to renew their courage, hope, and aspiration. They responded especially when he would take the hand of a discouraged lad and say: "I understand, Son. You know, I'm blind, too." Sometimes our grief can heighten our ability to understand and help others when they have a need.

A woman in England had lived for many years on the southeastern coast where chalk cliffs rose perpendicularly out of the sea. One night she dreamed she was climbing up the face of the cliffs by clinging to iron stakes which were set in the mountainside.

Hand over hand she climbed up the cliffside until her strength began to fail just as she drew close to the top. She felt that her strength had gone and despair overtook her as she felt unable to climb any higher. Afraid to look down, she looked up and suddenly she saw a great hand stretched toward her which grasped her and lifted her up to safety. The dream provided needed assurance for this woman, because life had been difficult for her and she had tried to meet her problems with only her own strength. Your presence can be for a friend the needed hand to help him climb over the mountainside of grief and suffering to a place where he can stand firmly. Be there.

Allow the griever opportunity to talk and take time to listen to him. Talking out his grief or speaking about the mixed feelings which he has about the deceased provides the bereaved person an occasion to release "bottled up" emotions. Learn to be a good listener. Don't tell him: "Don't talk about it. It will only make you feel worse." Now it may make you feel worse if you are not strong enough yourself to receive the emotional release which the griever may sometimes unleash. The bereaved usually wants to talk about his loss, but some well-meaning friends may say: "Well, I wanted to let you know how I felt, but I knew I would break down in front of you if I did. So, I just didn't come." What difference would that make! Your friend may be strengthened by your expression of grief for him, and your show of emotions will help him realize that he, too, can express his feelings openly. Talking about the dead person may be the very best thing for the bereaved person to do.

An older man who had lost his wife talked to me about how careless and indifferent some people acted since the death of his wife. "They would meet me on the street for the first time since my wife's death," he said, "and never even mention it. They would talk about everything else but that. I guess they thought if they talked to me about it, it would hurt me. But it really hurt a lot more for them to act as though nothing had happened at all." A man whose son had been killed in an automobile accident complained: "My friends would drop by the house to see me and say, 'I'm sorry,' and then sit down and turn the conversation to the weather, sports, church, politics, etc. I wanted to yell out and say: 'Talk to me about my son! This is no social call!' Why is it so difficult for people to talk about death?"

If we do not give the griever an opportunity or make him feel he can express his emotions, he may withdraw, believing he has been rejected, or push the feelings deep down inside himself which may cause him emotional or physical damage later. Be willing to listen and not judge. Feelings of all kind may pour out—expressions of guilt, neglect, hostility, fear, self-pity, depression, or rejection. If you furnish a sounding board which bereaved friends can use to talk out their feelings, it will be more therapeutic than you can ever imagine. "Well has it been said," wrote Henry Wadsworth Longfellow, "that there is no grief like the grief which does not speak." Dietrich Bonhoeffer was certainly correct when he observed: "He who can no longer listen to his brother will soon be no longer listening to God either; he will be doing nothing but prattle in the presence of God, too." [7]

Let your bereaved friend express his emotions. Be a person with whom the griever can weep unashamedly, knowing that you are suffering with him. Sustain him in his need to express his sorrow. Many times a friend will mistakenly say: "Oh, don't cry; it will be all right." Our society has put a taboo on any external sign of emotion at the funeral service or before people. Tears are often seen as evidence of weakness or one's inability to deal with the situation. Tears are supposed to be a sign of weakness or of an effeminate nature; any outward display of emotion is taken to be a degrading or demeaning characteristic. Who can really judge what gave birth to such a false view of life?

A stoical attitude is usually the one that receives the greatest praise from well-meaning friends: "Oh, you are being so brave." "You are taking it so well." "How wonderful you are not to let this throw you." Instead of this unreal pretense in the light of one's loss, we need to encourage the right of the grief-sufferer to mourn. Grief, as Edgar Jackson has observed, is "an honorable emotion," and everyone has the right and should be allowed the privilege of this honest emotion. Many of our modern funeral homes have perpetuated this taboo attitude regarding any emotional expression of grief by placing the mourners behind a screen or in a private room off to the side of the chapel. This infers that there is something bad or unacceptable about public expression of grief.

Modern society likes to ridicule the old-fashioned wakes and ancient customs of burial and mourning rites. Their functions, which often served as a real outlet for experiences of grief have now been replaced with sleeping pills, tranquilizers, stimulants, alcohol, or other evasive means of escaping the reality of what has really happened. Modern man's denial of weeping is a poisonous infection in the blood stream of modern life. Tears have been called "the safety valves of the heart when too much pressure is laid on it." I wonder if the young mother who said that she was complimented for acting like a zombie at the death of her child would have taken her own life if her friends had permitted her the normal release of her emotions instead of praising her for such unnatural behavior.

John Sutherland Bonnell makes reference to a young doctor and his wife who came to talk with him about some marital problems.[8] "There is something wrong with our marriage and there always has been," said the doctor. "I love my wife very dearly and I hope she loves me, but there seems to be some barrier in her life that keeps her from entering wholeheartedly into our marriage. She seems to build up a wall against me. Our marriage has never been really happy either physically or spiritually. I am hoping that there is something you can tell us that will help to change this situation." The young wife broke down, weeping, and said: "I know I don't love my husband as I ought to. I try to but something holds me back."

After five or six interviews, Dr. Bonnell noted that the wife recalled many memories from her childhood and they were all closely associated with her father. She had been very close to her father, the apple of his eye. He often played with her, and she would sit for long periods on his lap. When the doctor's wife was only eight years old, and while she was away visiting a relative, her father suddenly died, and they did not bring her home until after the funeral. Without the presence of her father the child was completely lost and brokenhearted, and, although they told her that he had died, she had not experienced death in any way and the word was meaningless to her. She felt repulsed and rejected by her mother and later by her stepfather who only tolerated her. Throughout her teenage and college years and even into her period of engagement, marriage, and birth of her children, she continued to sustain a mental image of her father as though he were still living and that somewhere she would one day find him again.

Dr. Bonnell observed: "She couldn't give herself completely to her husband because her father was still her first love. She felt that loyalty and devotion to him demanded that everybody else in her life would have a secondary place. This fact she would have to see and understand for herself; not only had she to grasp it intellectually but it had to penetrate into her feelings. She had to know in her deepest being that her father had died and that in her lifetime she would never see him again."

Dr. Bonnell then talked to the young woman about death and unresolved grief. Later he received a call from her very disturbed husband: "What is happening with my wife?" he asked. "For two nights in succession she has cried almost all night long, sobbing till her whole body is shaking. I am very much alarmed. Has something gone wrong in the counseling?" Dr. Bonnell assured him that nothing was wrong but that this was the belated grief of his wife on behalf of her father and to let her continue until her weeping ended on its own. After several more interviews with Dr. Bonnell, the young wife learned to transfer her affection from her dead father to her husband. "Our marriage now," the doctor called later to say, "is filled with a happiness that we have never known before. It is as though we are on our honeymoon. We have a joy and happiness in each other that is beyond measure."

Why should anyone feel ashamed of crying in the face of sorrow?

Tears are the avenue of expression which God has given to us to release the pent-up emotions which, if unresolved, may distort our very personality with the power of their internal agitation. "There is a sacredness in tears," Washington Irving once penned. "They are not the mark of weakness but of power. They speak more eloquently than ten thousand tongues. They are the messengers of overwhelming grief, of deep contrition, and of unspeakable love." Another voice, that of the poet Leigh Hunt, expressed it this way: "God made both tears and laughter, and both for kind purpose; for as laughter enables mirth and surprise to breathe freely, so tears enable sorrow to vent itself patiently."

Permit your bereaved friend the occasion he needs and allow him to weep. Do so with understanding, compassion, and acceptance. Some claim the only verse from the New Testament they can quote is "Jesus wept." Urge them to remember it and weep with the knowledge that Jesus said: "Blessed are they that mourn; for they shall be comforted" (Matt. 5:4, KJV).

Stick by your grieving friend with your continuous support. When death first strikes the home, the blow is so stunning that it results in shock. Through these days of initial grief and the funeral service, we are often anesthetized and only later does the awesome reality of what has happened slowly begin to dawn upon us. During this later period of adjustment your friend may need you more then than he ever did. He longs for a sense of acceptance, support, encouragement, and love. Support him with your presence, your concern, your interest, and devotion. Words may sometimes fail you, but a tangible act may express your supportive presence. You can bring a pie and sit and listen for awhile. You can drop in for coffee or bring a new recipe if your friend is a grieving widow. Invite her over for a snack or to go shopping with you or to attend your church with you. Help your widower friend by an invitation over for a meal, or to watch television with you, or to play a round of golf, or to go fishing.

In many small ways, you can keep a continual interest expressed to your friend to let him know you care and feel with him. The apostle Paul said every man was a minister; the only distinction is functional. Your pastor is limited in the amount of time he can give to any one person, but the church's ministry can continue to reach out to touch the life of a bereaved person as you minister to him as an extension of Christ's ministry. "Bear one another's burdens, and so fulfil the law of Christ" (Gal. 6:2).

The Christian community has been called, according to Bonhoeffer, to the "ministry of helpfulness." Sometimes we must assist in trivial, trifling, petty affairs which may interrupt our schedules and direct us to the meanest of services. "We must be ready to allow ourselves to be interrupted by God," Bonhoeffer noted. "God will be constantly crossing our paths and canceling our plans by sending us people with claims and petitions." [9] The Christian, as Bonhoeffer understood him, had been called to suffer with and bear the burden of his fellowman. "It is only when he is a burden that another person is really a brother and not merely an object to be manipulated." [10]

Several years ago Ted Husing, a popular and successful radio announcer, had a brain operation that left him blind, paralyzed, and his speech partially impaired.[11] His suffering and condition made him very bitter, and he refused to see anyone except his wife, daughter, and mother. While he was in the hospital, he left strict orders that none of his friends were to be told where he was, but some of them found out and came to visit him. They continued to come, although he rebuffed and insulted them.

His friends persisted until finally one was able to persuade him to attend a baseball game where he might have a chance to hear the crack of a bat against a ball and smell the aroma of hot dogs and peanuts. "Ted," his friend whispered to him, "you are going to make it with the help of God." Ted had become very bitter toward God because of his ailment but the faith of his friend and the flood of mail from people all across the United States who indicated their prayerful concern for him fortified and rebuilt his faith in God.

With a measure of his health regained, Ted dreams of returning one day to his radio work. The biggest lesson he learned, he stated, was that a man needs his friends, and he cannot exist meaningfully independent of them. "I am grateful," he reflects, "when I consider that through the goodness of undeserved friends, God became a loving reality for me."

Undergird your friends in their grief with the assurance that your friendship is a durable knot and it can withstand the strains, shocks, and calamities which may pull against it. "The test of friendship," Gandhi said, "is assistance in adversity, and that, too, unconditional assistance. Co-operation which needs consideration is a commercial contract and not friendship. Conditional co-operation is like adulterated cement which does not bind."

Guide your bereaved friend, as the occasion arises, to direct his grief toward some positive end. When Paul and Silas found themselves chained in prison, the book of Acts reveals that they began to sing praises and pray to God at midnight. In the midnight of their adversity they reached out for the presence of God and directed their calamity to be used by God. This is seldom easy to do; it is easier to complain, brood over your situation, express bitterness, feel depressed, mourn at your privation, or feel despondent about your loss.

At some point in one's experience with grief, he must rise above the lower moods that want to imprison him, lift up his voice and sing praises, and pray to God in the midnight of his sorrow. You, as a friend, may be able to help direct him to this sense of release and renewed vision on life. "Every man has his Bethlehem where new possibilities and hopes are born," Sam Keen affirms, "where his history is invaded by novelty and the potency for new action. At such times the tyranny of the past and the terror of the future give way before a new time of open possibility—the vibrant present." [12] When that vibrant present breaks before the bereaved, or even before the light comes, he needs to "lose his grief" in unselfish service to others who sorrow or have manifold needs.

Once the bereaved has realistically faced and accepted his loss, then he needs to direct his new sensitivity into meaningful service. This kind of activity is more than just busyness to avoid facing the loss; the death has already been faced and now the griever turns to find his role again in society. But this time he goes into life with a new awareness about the gift of life and its value and the reality and pain of separation. With this new insight, his grief can cause him to turn inward and long for pity or turn outward and search for ways to help others.

I read about a wealthy woman who loaded her car with exquisite flowers each Sunday and was driven to her son's grave where she would place the flowers on his grave. This weekly ritual became her only reason for living. On one visit she became so weak that she almost fainted and the gardener at the cemetery caught her before she collapsed. "Why do you put yourself through this every week?" the gardener asked tenderly. "I watched you for so long and just ached to talk to you. But I was afraid." "Afraid of me?" she asked with unbelief. "Yes, of hurting your feelings," he answered. "Look just beyond this cemetery. See that hospital over there? Why don't you take his flowers to them each Sunday? There are boys over there who never have a flower on their table. I see them hanging out the window to see the lilacs here when they come in bloom." Her spirit still sick within, she looked up at the dim figures in pajamas on the porches—"I'll send them flowers," she answered. "Oh, no," the old gardener replied. "Go yourself, ma'am. Bring them his flowers each Sunday—let them see your smile when you give them. Promise."

Later instead of placing flowers on the grave of a dead son, she was seen by the gardener, even during the World War II gasoline shortage, pedaling her bicycle loaded with flowers through the hospital gates to the young patients. Afterwards she would return and tell the gardener about the patients she had visited.

Many have lost sons or daughters, husbands or wives, mothers or fathers to dread diseases like cancer or leukemia, as well as useless accidents. Instead of floundering in their grief, some have chosen avenues to promote research; provided funds to build children's homes; established grants for medical students; or contributed large or small sums to better the conditions of man. Help your friend direct his grief toward a positive end which can accomplish something. "It is better to light a candle than to curse the darkness."

Help the bereaved sense the inner resources which can sustain him during his time of grief. The Christian affirms the reality of a presence which sustains him in the midst of the crises of life. Some feel it strongly; others search for it in vain; while others find it only gradually in their sorrow. C. S. Lewis who was a professor of literature both at Oxford and Cambridge was an agnostic before he became a devout Christian.

One of the great trials in his life came after the death of his beloved wife who had shared his life for only a few years. Shortly after her death he began to jot down in a notebook some of his feelings about her death. At first one notes a sense of shock, frustration, and bitterness against God and life, but then gradually you observe a turning again to the presence of God. Lewis declared: "You never know how much you really believe anything until its truth or falsehood becomes a matter of life and death to you." [13] He observed that a person might believe that a rope is strong and sound if he merely needs it to tie up a box but if he had to hang over a precipice with it, then he would discover how much he really trusted it. Suffering, sorrow, and death are often our greatest precipice experiences of life's testing.

John R. Claypool a minister who lost his young daughter a few years ago to leukemia was confronted by a friend who inquired: "Give it to me straight. I am not asking you this as a preacher. I am asking you as an honest human being. Was there anybody or anything down there at the bottom? When the chips were really down, does this 'thing' we call God really make any difference?" Knowing his friend too well to put up a front or offer a pat answer, John thought and answered: "Yes I can honestly say there was Something there in the darkness. The mystery of Goodness was present. I was given help. It was not the sort of thing I have heard other people talk about when they were in deep circumstances, and yet, for me, it was very real." He then went on and shared how the passage from Isaiah 40:27-31 had been crucial in the understanding of his experience. "I can report

honestly," John continued, "that strength 'to walk and not faint'
was given. No ecstasy. No great energy. Just the gift of endur-
ance—that was all that met me in the depths of darkness. I did
not soar with wings or run a step. But by the grace of God,
somehow I stayed on my feet." [14]

With the coming of grief each man tests the fibers of his own
rope of faith. As a Christian, we meet it with the conquering
assurance of the Christ who says: "Because I live, ye shall live
also." We meet it also with the words of Paul ringing in our
ears. "We know that in everything God works for good with
those who love him, who are called according to his purpose.
Who shall separate us from the love of Christ? Shall tribulation,
or distress, or persecution, or famine, or nakedness, or peril, or
sword? No, in all these things we are more than conquerors
through him that loved us. For I am sure that neither death,
nor life, nor angels, nor principalities, nor things present, nor
things to come, nor powers, nor height, nor depth, nor anything
else in all creation, will be able to separate us from the love
of God in Christ Jesus our Lord" (Rom. 8:28,35,37-38).

We confront grief again with the assurance of the promises
of Jesus, "So you have sorrow now, but I will see you again and
your hearts will rejoice, and no one will take your joy from you"
(John 16:22). "Peace I leave with you; my peace I give to you;
not as the world gives do I give to you. Let not your hearts
be troubled, neither let them be afraid" (John 14:27).

A young boy was helping his father bring in some wood for
the fire, and he was struggling under the weight of a heavy load.
"Why don't you use all your strength?" the father asked. "I am,"
the little lad responded, feeling dejected. "No you're not," declared
the father, "You have not asked me to help you." And he reached
down and lifted up both the boy and log in his arms. No one
has ever used all his strength until he has drawn on the source
of all strength itself—the eternal God. "Cast your burden on the
Lord, and he will sustain you" (Ps. 55:22).

4
Death and the Meaning of Life

The first impact of *The Persistence of Memory*, a painting by Salvador Dali, is a haunting one. The absolute bleakness seems overpowering. Broken and bent watches are seen lying against a dull, drab background. One distorted watch appears to be folded over a bare table which has a barren tree jutting forth from it with a sagging watch hanging limply over a single dead limb. Another watch is lying on the table covered with insects apparently feasting on it. On the barren ground lies something like a rolled-up blanket, or a dead animal, with a watch bent in a folded, twisted fashion over it. In the background is an empty sky and a desolate mountain. The lifeless watches and the forlorn images in the painting reflect a philosophy which sees death as waste or ruin, and the title itself denotes the wretchedness of one trying to live in past memories. Death invades not only the past but the present as a waster and destroyer of life. The painting seems to depict death as that awesome force which rejects time as having any meaning for man.

The German philosopher Martin Heidegger, who struggled with the theme of death in many of his major works, noted, "Death is a way of being which takes over transience as soon as it is. As soon as a man begins to live, he is old enough to die." "The whole life of the philosopher," Plato observed, "is a preparation for death." The Reformation leader Martin Luther declared: "The summons of death comes to us all, and no one can die for another. Everyone must fight his own battle with death by himself alone."

All of them have stated the issue: The question of death raises the question of the meaning of life. Albert Camus once said that "Man cannot live without meaning." The way one sees death determines the way one understands life's meaning. When the awesome reality of death finally breaks in upon us, the biggest question of our existence is raised. Does life have meaning? The ultimate answer to that question is our conclusion about death. Everything in nature dies. An insect, a bird, a fish, a fox, a tree; they will die like man. But the distinction man holds over them is that he knows he will one day die, and the others are unaware of it. This is both his advantage and despair, blessing and curse, because unlike the rest of nature which also dies, man alone is able to anticipate his demise. How, then, are we to live in the awareness of death? Several voices clamor for attention.

Does Death Destroy All Meaning?

Loud outcries are raised by some who envision death as denying all meaning to life. Death is the great scandal. Only negation, despair, nothingness, senselessness, and restlessness result from its hold on life. Life is merely a charade, and man drinks from the cup of life what he can while moving quickly onward without purpose or direction, unable to avoid the rapid torrents of annihilation which summon him. This philosophy was echoed by Shakespeare's Macbeth, "Out, out, brief candle! Life's but a walking shadow."

Heidegger, Karl Jasper, Jean-Paul Sartre, and other existential philosophers acknowledge this sense of nothingness in life and the dread it projects for man's existence, but their conclusion is that there is no final consolation, no immortality. Life ends shipwrecked on the rock of death which carries man to the chilling depths of nonbeing. Man's inner feelings of restlessness, his disturbing sense of estrangement from himself, his neighbor, and his world—this nameless fear is the fear of death. What the existentialists call man's sense of aloneness, his feelings of isolation, his awareness of finitude, and the inevitability of death is acknowledged as man's knowledge of the absolute end of existence at death.

Others like Camus and Ernest Hemingway filled their writings with man's confrontation with death, suffering, pain, and depravity in a desperate effort to come to grips with the question of meaning. Drawing upon the Spanish influence of Miguel de Unamuno, Hemingway used the Spanish word for nothing, *nada*, and has one of his characters pray, "Our *nada*, which art in *nada*." The "Ave Maria" is transposed to say, "Hail, *nada*, full of *nada*."

The contemporary "theater of the absurd" depicts this fatalistic outlook in the plays of Edward Albee, Eugene Ionesco, Samuel Beckett, and others. Illusion and reality lose their distinction as men and women become insects, change into rhinoceroses, wait endlessly, use nonsense language, or are tyrannized by a universe which seems to have gone mad. Everything falls apart because life is without meaning at the very core of existence.

For some the fog has not lifted. They see no way out; the street is a dead end; the path ends at a precipice; the ship is sucked under by the vortex; the sleep of death is unending.

Charles Shulz in his *Peanuts* comic strip may have reflected the feelings of some of us about this philosophy of life. Charlie Brown and Lucy are seen talking behind a brick wall. Charlie states, "Someone has said that we should live each day as if it were the last day of our life." Lucy's reaction to this comment is interesting. "Aaugh! This is the last day!! This is it!!! I only have twenty-four hours left! Help me! Help me! This is the last day! Aaugh!" Leaning on one elbow, Charlie Brown, now alone, observes, "Some philosophies aren't for all people." [1] How true it is. The way of despair does not have to be our philosophy for life. Other possibilities are open to us.

The Deadly Practice of Nonliving

Maybe worse than a sense of futility about death is to be unaware that one is alive. Many of us remember the prayer that we used to pray as a small child. "Now I lay me down to sleep, I pray thee, Lord, my soul to keep; If I should die before I wake, I pray, thee, Lord, my soul to take." Someone may have stumbled on the deeper meaning of the line, "if I should die before I wake," when he carried it through to say "if I should die before I wake up to live." The poet Rilke has caught this lesson in his refrain,

"The deadliest death of all is to be alive and not to know it."

On a visit to New York City, Henry David Thoreau made this observation: "I walked through New York yesterday—and met no real and living person." Some go through life as dead persons. Each day is greeted only with boredom, depression, loneliness, apathy, insensitivity, disinterest, and meaningless routine. These people exist but are not alive; they breathe but do not comprehend; they stare but do not see; hear without listening, touch without feeling, taste without savor. They move through life, but little of life moves through them. They remain detached, remote, unmoved, uninvolved. Life is hardly a spectator's sport to them. Life is spent rushing, as it were, from one store to the other without making any purchases. Time is consumed by rushing to one vestibule after another, without ever going in to see the play, enjoy the show, observe the film, participate in the game. Life for them is a waiting game. They are always waiting for something better to come along to claim their attention. But they only wait; they never respond to the life already around them. They wait and wait and wait. "I used to think that people only died when they were put in coffins," Laura said, in Ellen Glasgow's *The Wheel of Life*, "but I know now that you can be dead and yet move and walk about and even laugh and pretend to be like all the rest—some of whom are dead also." [2]

Hardly a day passes without some transient coming by the church seeking a handout or a bus ticket to another city. To many of these men and women this has become just a way of life. They move from church to church and from city to city, living like parasites off whatever they can beg or solicit. Many of them are alcoholics and live on the edge of hunger and poverty all of their lives. They simply pass through life. They merely exist from one day to the next without thought, purpose, or meaning except for a bit of bread, another drink, a cheap or free bed, and a free trip to the next town. In this endless circle they live out their lives.

Two tragic stories illustrate the deadly practice of nonliving. Several years ago in one of the large metropolitan cities a well-known street beggar was found dead in his run-down room in a shabby hotel. The room looked like a city dump with its piles of dirty rags, old empty bottles, and broken bits of furniture barely hanging together. The beggar was clothed only in rags, his body was filthy from months without bathing, and his face bore a beard which was rarely shaved. When the dirty mattress on which the beggar was lying dead was accidentally opened, thousands of dollars were discovered buried in that mattress bank. This man, who had lived his life in poverty and filth, was, all the time, hoarding a small fortune in his room. But he died without using his wealth to help himself or others.

Luigi Corneglio lived and died in a similar fashion. He was known by his outstretched hand and pauper's existence. However, when he died at seventy in a dirty, cheap tenement house, his attic contained forty-seven violins, one of which was a priceless Stradivarius. He died surrounded by musical instruments, one of them invaluable, without the resounding beauty of the music within them finding life and response from a caring touch or responsive ear. The Stradivarius violin was not meant for a dusty attic but was made to share beautiful music with mankind. Neither was life meant to be lived in miserly, poverty existence but in notes of joy, beauty, responsiveness, celebration, and creativity.

Man is given freedom by his creator to choose the level of existence on which he wants to live his life. The gift of life is never to be taken lightly. Every life is important in its potential and vitality. Pascal reminded us that "The least movement is of importance to all nature. The entire ocean is affected by a pebble." "No man should think himself a zero," observed Bernard Baruch, "and think he can do nothing about the state of the world."

Turn now in your mind and look at two other lives. One of the twentieth-century's greatest men was Albert Schweitzer. This remarkable man had, it seemed, limitless gifts which he dedicated to the service of God and mankind. When he had already been recognized as a brilliant theologian, philosopher, organist, musicologist, professor, and minister, he turned his life away from dazzling world acclaim and prepared himself to serve as a medical missionary in Africa. One day a friend cautioned him that one could not burn a candle at both ends. Schweitzer responded by saying, "You can if the candle is long enough!" Instead of turning his life inward with concern only for his selfish goals, he extended his life and gifts outward to embrace the world with service and sacrifice.

Schweitzer believed that he should make some acknowledgement to God for the happiness he had experienced through his study and through his work in science and art. He awoke one morning with the realization: "I must not accept this happiness as a matter of course, but must give something in return for it . . . I tried to settle what meaning lay hidden for me in the saying of Jesus! 'Whosoever would save his life shall lose it, and whosoever shall lose his life for My sake and the Gospel's shall save it.' Now the answer was found. In addition to the outward, I now had inward happiness." [3]

On the other hand, no life could have looked less promising than that of Helen Keller. At eighteen months of age illness shut out her world, and she became blind and deaf. Through the gifted work of her teacher, Anne Sullivan, Helen Keller not only learned to "read," write, and talk but graduated from college and inspired the world with her courage, wisdom, faith, and insight. She once observed that only those who have lost some of their senses really appreciate them. Only the deaf really appreciate hearing and the blind realize the blessing of sight.

In a casual walk through the woods, a person with all of his senses on being asked what he saw might respond, "nothing in particular." Through her touch alone in a walk through the woods, Miss Keller could "see" the delicate symmetry of a leaf, the smooth skin of a silver birch, the rough shaggy bark of a pine, the velvety texture of a flower, or "hear" the song of a bird through the touch of her hand on a small tree as it quivered from the vibration of the happy bird in song.

I who am blind can give one hint to those who see: use your eyes as if tomorrow you would be stricken blind. And the same method can be applied to the other senses. Hear the music of voices, the song of a bird, the mighty strains of an orchestra, as if you would be stricken deaf tomorrow. Touch each object you want to touch as if tomorrow your tactile sense would fail. Smell the perfume of flowers, taste with relish each morsel, as if tomorrow you could never smell and taste again. Make the most of every sense; glory in all the facets of pleasure and beauty.[4]

In these two lives—Helen Keller and Albert Schweitzer—see the gift of life used to its fullness.

The Certainty of Death Enhances the Significance of Life

Sometimes we like to speculate on what we would do if we thought our physical life here on this planet would never come to an end. Would that really be a blessing or might it not be, on the other hand, a curse. An ancient Greek myth illustrates the curse that endless living might entail in its account of the love story of the goddess of the dawn, Aurora, and her romance with a mortal man named Tithonus. Zeus, the king of the gods, lends his support to this love affair and offers Aurora any gift she desires for her lover. She asked that Tithonus be granted to live forever, but she forgot to ask that he might also have the gift of eternal youth. As a goddess, Aurora remained young, but Tithonus continued to grow older and could not die. Life soon became for him an ordeal and burden of torture and difficulty. He longed for death.

"The inevitability of death accepted at the highest level of passion," Kierkegaard declared, "is an empowering thing." Instead of shattering all meaning from life, death can be the driving force that compels us to see the significance of life. The very fact that each of us knows that he or she will not live forever here, should force us to confront the question: "What am I doing with the gift of life I have now?"

Without the reality and certainty of death, I wonder when we would finally confront the reason for our own existence. Death gives significance to our lives because we know there is a termination point. We are all such terrible procrastinators as it is. Can you imagine how long it would be before some of us got around to educating ourselves, securing a job, starting a home and family if we thought we would never die? Would we ever cease our playing and postponement? Why do so many writers, artists, musicians, poets, inventors, scientists, and others work with such a driving compulsion? The knowledge of approaching death and the shortness of time gives a greater sense of urgency to the work of any person. Since death will end man's labor here, some work against time and death itself to acquire a kind of immortal fame.

In his novel *The Idiot,* Dostoyevsky tells of a young man facing the sentence of death. He, like all of us, did not want to be cut off in the prime of life.

He said that nothing was so dreadful at that time as the continual thought, 'What if I were not to die! What if I could go back to life—what eternity! And it would be all mine! I would turn every minute into an age; I would lose nothing. I would count every minute as it passed, I would not waste one!' He said that this idea turned to such a fury at last that he longed to be shot quickly.[5]

Often when a person has had a heart attack, faced dangerous surgery, been in an accident, been under fire from enemy bullets in time of war, come close to drowning, or known some other peril, he will make promises about how he is going to live with more awareness of time, a deeper commitment to God, and greater concern for others. Sometimes we mean these words, and some few do fulfill their wish, but most forget the good intentions when they are well again and busy in their jobs and other activities. The finality of death does stab us awake to the limitations of time which are imposed upon each of us. The proper stewardship of time, then, is more than a much-used cliche.

How aware are we of the significance of time? Everyone has the same amount of time, every day, twenty-four hours—no more, no less. The beggars who pass through our church have the same amount of time which the President of the United States has. Everyone of us has 168 hours in a week. If I work 56 of these hours, sleep 56 hours, eat for 12 of them, I still have 44 hours left out of every week. What do most of us do with those forty-four hours? Most of us would have difficulty explaining to others where the time goes. It eludes us.

Even with all of our "timesaving" devices, we still cannot save time. It is something that cannot be put in a bank; it cannot be hoarded in a secret container; it does not stand still for anyone. One day a small girl heard her mother, who was weary from running from one place to another with the children, exclaim, "Where does the time go?" "Why mother," she replied, "the time goes into all the things you do." And so it does.

When I was a boy I thought I would never get to high school. In high school I thought the time would never arrive when I would be in college. In college I longed for the time to be finished with school and seminary and into life. As I think back now, I wonder how much time I wasted spending so much of my thoughts and energy anticipating something to come in the future and did not live fully in the present. So much of our time is literally wasted in yearning too much for tomorrow and not learning to live in the present. When we are very young, we feel we have a lifetime to get our education; we cannot understand our parents' insistence that we get on with it. When we are first married, we feel we have a lifetime to raise our children, but before we know it they are grown and married themselves. Where does time go? It goes into everything we do—our work, play, sleep, eating, worship, daydreams, yearnings, idleness, service, misbehavior, moods—it penetrates all of our living.

Time is the most precious ingredient of life we possess. Death has a positive value of forcing us to an awareness of the brevity of life and to the summons to "spend" it carefully and wisely. The psalmist has urged us to remember: "The years of our life are threescore and ten, or even by reason of strength fourscore; . . . they are soon gone, and we fly away. So teach us to number our days that we may get a heart of wisdom" (Ps. 90:10,12). When one has learned to live with the awareness of death and the fact that death can interrupt life at any moment, time and life take on a deeper meaning. One then values life not merely in terms of its length but by the quality of the intensity by which one has attempted to live those moments he has had opportunity to touch.

Length alone does not become the proper criterion for judging the significance of a life. Methuselah lived to be nine hundred and sixty-nine years old, but in his almost thousand years of life the only noteworthy thing was the list of his children. The artist Raphael died at thirty-six; John Keats the poet died at twenty-four; Frederick W. Robertson the English preacher was only thirty-seven at his death. Many others have died at a relatively young age—Dr. Tom Dooley, Abraham Lincoln, John Kennedy, Martin Luther King, Jr. Length of life was not the factor that determined their usefulness and contribution. If they had lived longer, the contributions of each may have been greater, but each made a significant contribution to the service of mankind. Even Jesus Christ was only thirty-three when he died. His accomplishment is not judged by only the length of his life. The quality of living often may far outstrip the quantity of a life.

You and I, as urbanized, modern folks, do not have to milk the cow and feed the pigs, chickens, and other animals before breakfast. We do not bring water in from the well for drinking or cooking or heat it to bathe in. We don't split the firewood, grow our own crops for food, raise our own sheep for wool, read by kerosene lantern, salt our meat to preserve it, or the thousand other chores our parents or grandparents had to do. In the light of all the "extra" time our modern gadgets have freed us to have, where does the time go? With all the "timesaving" devices we now possess, what significant things will we do with the time we have saved? It's one of those pesty questions that will not go away.

If you knew you were going to die at the end of this year, or at the end of this month, or at the end of this week, what would be your priorities? What would be the things which you would seek to give your attention to more than anything else in the light of your approaching death? We need to ask that question of ourselves, because soon all of us will die—maybe not

next year, or next month, nor next week but one day. Our selection
of priorities, what we consider important, will determine how
we spend our time.

In Thornton Wilder's play *Our Town*, Emily Gibbs, who died
giving birth to her baby, is granted an opportunity to come back
and visit earth and observe the celebration of the child's twelfth
birthday with her family. At first, as she watches herself and her
family at breakfast, she is overjoyed; but suddenly in her observation of the reliving of a portion of her past, she realizes that
in everyone's busyness, no one is really paying much attention
to each other. In her sadness Emily cries out: "Oh, earth, you're
too wonderful for anyone to realize you. Do any human beings
ever realize life while they live it?—every, every minute?" She
asks the stage manager through her tears. "No," he responds, "The
Saints and Poets, maybe—they do some." [6]

Death and the Testing of Silence

Death appears to cross the path of our lives and sever our
chord of attachment to all that we consider important, worthwhile,
meaningful, and lovable. Death seems to come as the final contradiction of the meaningfulness of our existence. Does death shatter
all of our dreams and hopes and shout shrilly the final finis for
us all, "That's all there is?" The last sentence in Tolstoy's great
novel *War and Peace* concludes not with a final period, indicating
the termination point, but instead trails off with three dots. Maybe
these three dots, which reveal that all has not been said, can
be seen as a lesson also about death—all has not been said when
it speaks its word. More words are yet to come. Words that may
rewrite, redirect, alter, modify, change, cancel, delete, erase,
obliterate, or transform what appears to be the last word.

Paul Tournier in a warm and moving book *Learn to Grow Old*
deals with the meaning of death as the religious question par
excellence. Dr. Tournier faces the question, "Can I as a Christian
accept death?" He responds to his own question by saying, "I
cannot honestly reply anything other than 'Yes and No.' What
a contradiction! I am very much afraid that will disappoint many

of my readers, who expect solid affirmation from a Christian. But the contradiction lies at the heart of our human nature." Tournier's struggle is what every man experiences in the light of life and death. Yes, in some way we can accept death—in faith, but some rebellion remains because of our unwillingness to relinquish our hold on life. While Tournier was in the midst of the writing of this book, his wife raised a question: "Are you getting on all right with your book? Where have you got up to?" "I'm still at death," Tournier answered. "Aren't you going to get to resurrection soon?" she asked. "I know what she means!" he replied. "But resurrection does not do away with death. It follows it. I cannot minimize death because I believe in resurrection. Even the tragedy of Good Friday only had the intensity it had because Christ was really and exclusively experiencing death, and not, in anticipation, his resurrection, the mystery of which was still in God." [7] Jesus Christ first faced his own death, and he faced it as we do, with faith and then came resurrection.

So we approach death with a yes—a faith, but a strong no of nagging doubt still remains. We want absolute, positive assurance, but it does not come in that kind of a package. It comes in a commitment of life, a trusting faith in the living Christ. Only in the experience of death itself can we truly know the depth of our commitment and the assuring presence of God. We take the step into the unknown by faith—not by absolute knowledge—only after the step has been taken do we *know*. A line from one of William Faulkner's short stories states well this struggle. "A man can see so much further when he stands in the darkness than he does when, standing in the light, he tries to probe the darkness." Maybe it is true; only those who have experienced the darkness of death or grief can testify to the character of the surrounding light.

In the agonizing mystery of death the Christian "waits on the Word of God in silence," wrote Thomas Merton. "And when he is 'answered,' it is not so much by a word that bursts into his silence. It is by his silence itself suddenly, inexplicably revealing itself to him as a word of great power, full of the voice of God." [8]

Again he said: "But for us the mystery contains, within its own darkness and its own silences, a presence and a meaning which we apprehend without fully understanding them." [9] Death always brings the testing of silence. We learn to listen for the presence of gentle stillness in the midst of the sounds of silence.

Dr. William Hull, professor of New Testament theology at the Southern Baptist Theological Seminary in Louisville, Kentucky, recounted an experience which he and his wife had as they sat with a minister friend and his family during the last few hours before his friends lost their young daughter to leukemia. At sunset the end came and an indescribable silence settled on the house. Earlier in the day sobs of pain and the sounds of attentive parents had filled the house. Now the sounds of suffering were over. Dr. Hull reflected that he knew that his friends would not hear again their young daughter's laughter or the dancing step of a young girl awaiting her first date. The test of silence fell that afternoon upon their house to see if it could be endured. "The silence lasted 'for about half an hour,' " Dr. Hull remarked, "as the family said good-bye. When they came down, there was really nothing to say, nor is there now. Except that the seemingly endless half hour of silence is in heaven, too. And I knew that afternoon that the silence could be endured. For the silence belongs to God."

The testing of silence comes to us all. None escape it. In the coming of the silence, we long for the disclosure of an abiding presence which no man can take away from us. In the testing of the silence, we await the final disclosure of the meaning of death by the one who is the Creator of life itself. Even in the coming of death, we feel in this silence still a pull toward the future; the more than; the yet to be said word, which only a living God can say.

"It was not until after the coming of Christ that time and man could breathe freely." Nikolai said, in Boris Pasternak's *Dr. Zhivago,* "It was not until after Him that men began to *live toward the future.* Man does not die in a ditch like a dog—but at home in history, while the work toward the conquest of death is in full swing; he dies sharing in this work." [10]

5

The Mystery of Death

Leo Tolstoy recounts a curious Eastern fable which raises puzzling questions. In the story a traveler is attacked and pursued by savage animals, and in an attempt to save himself, he leaps into a dry well and clings to the branch of a wild plant growing on the wall of the well. Looking down he sees a dragon with its jaws wide open ready to devour him if he lets go of the branch. Although his arms are growing weary and he is aware that death awaits him on either side, he stubbornly holds on. Suddenly he notices two mice, one white and the other black, slowly gnawing the stem of the plant to which he is holding. He knows now even more that there is no hope, but suddenly he notices some drops of honey on the leaves of the plant, and he stretches out his tongue and licks them.[1]

Percy Bysshe Shelley says it disquietingly: "Life, like a dome of many colored glass, stains the white radiance of Eternity, until Death tramples it to fragments." There is no escaping it: death is the absolute question in life. Its insistent inquiry throbs within our heads, burning and twisting for a meaningful response. The Shakespearean query measures the authenticity of existence, "To be or not to be." But who can really conceive of himself as not existing? Unconsciousness, annihilation are fleeting thoughts that run through our minds but are as quickly dismissed as the mind can focus its attention on something else. "Each person is born," so stated Mark Twain, "to one possession which outvalues all the others—his last breath." Heidegger laid out the direction for other contemporary writers to follow in his influential view that life is primarily a "running forward to death."

Man cannot escape death; he is caught in its contradictory

undertow and he cannot help raising a "why?" Man is a "being unto death"—but death remains an annoying enigma which seems to have been savagely injected into the midst of life. Centuries ago Job raised his question, "If a man die shall he live again?" But there is no if—death is certain—all men will die, no one escapes death. There is a thirst within us which will remain eternally unsatisfied if death yanks the cup permanently away from the lips of our desires. We can agree, then, with the apostle Paul, "If in this life only we have hope in Christ, we are of all men most miserable" (1 Cor. 15:19, KJV).

Fully aware of the certainty of death, man has not been able to shake off the feeling of what George Santayana termed "the soul's invincible surmise." Everywhere and in every age man has been convinced that there is more to life than this brown, black, red, gray, yellow, orange clay. There has to be more! This thought most men have been unwilling to let go. Is this just wishful thinking, a dread of annihilation, an unrealistic hope, pious nonsense, "pie in the sky" religion, or cowardly behavior? Or—is there any possibility that death is not the end of man's existence? "Death is not a foe," declared Oliver Lodge, "but an inevitable adventure." Milton saw death as "the golden key that opens the palace of eternity." Most men have lived with this hope.

From the time of primitive, superstitious caveman to the lunar age, man has affirmed his belief that death is not the end. The Neanderthal man placed hunting and eating items with his dead to indicate his notion of the continuation of life; the Greeks dreamed of the Elysian Fields and the Isles of the Blest; the Egyptian pyramids are lasting monuments of another culture's belief in life after death. The Hebrews pictured life after death as a shadowy existence in Sheol. The American Indian had a vision of a happy hunting ground. The Polynesians saw the moon as their next world while the Mexicans and Peruvians pictured the sun as their future dwelling place. The fierce Norseman looked to his Valhalla; and the Mohammedan longed for a paradise of sensual satisfaction. In every age and culture man has attempted to affirm his belief in life after death.

The primitive expressions, childish notions, fantasized concepts, or worldly depictions may all prove to be inadequate, crude, unsophisticated, antiquated, or even unreal, but this will still not destroy the reality of anticipated life after death. Man may have certain ideas or symbols which he uses to try to convey his belief in a future beyond the grave, but its existence or nature is in no way determined by man's inadequate or puerile descriptions of it. No unborn child could imagine what the world outside the womb would be like; it has no way to make a comparison. No person born blind or deaf can really imagine the wonder of sight and sound. Man can project only from his known world, his hopes, his dreams, his aspirations.

Even the Christian, with the revelation he has through Jesus Christ, must be cautious in his language about what life after death is like. Paul expressed it vividly: "What no eye has seen, nor ear heard, nor the heart of man conceived, what God has prepared for those who love him" (1 Cor. 2:9). Joseph Addison said, " 'Tis heaven itself that points out an hereafter and intimates eternity to man." Maybe a nineteenth-century preacher, Frederick W. Robertson, has said it even better: "Every natural longing has its natural satisfaction. If we thirst, God has created liquids to gratify thirst. If we are susceptible of attachment, there are beings to gratify our love. If we thirst for life and love eternal, it is likely that there are an eternal life and an eternal love to satisfy that craving." [2]

The Mystery of Death

"I just do not understand it, pastor," the father said to me. "Why did my young son have to die? It just doesn't make any sense to me." Another—"He was only thirty years old and a brilliant German professor, why did he die instead of some useless bum on the street?" Still another—"She was so innocent and young. What did she do to deserve to die, pastor?" They join the chorus that cries out, "Why?" "Why?" If death is such a natural part of life, then why are we so unsatisfied with the answer that it is just the normal pattern when accidents occur, when cells and organs wear out or misfunction?

Have you had many doctors or ministers describe any death as just the natural thing to expect? If so, why should medical science work so laboriously to fight sickness and prolong life? The answer leaps at us—man senses that death is a contradiction which demands a deeper response. If death is merely a biological event in life, there is no mystery to it, and no darkness would then surround its coming. But for the Christian death is not simply a physiological fact. "Death proves to be the greatest paradox in the world, which cannot be understood rationally," Berdyaev said. "Death is folly that has become commonplace. The consciousness that death is an ordinary everyday occurrence has dulled our sense of its being irrational and paradoxical." [3]

Helmut Thielicke, a great German theologian and masterful preacher, recounts the following incident from the diary of a young pilot who was shot down in World War II. The pilot was gathering lilacs, and as he parted the branches of a flowering bush he came upon the half-decayed body of a soldier. For someone so young he had witnessed many deaths, and so he drew back in horror, not because he had never seen a dead body before but as a result of the frightful contradiction which he saw between the dead man and the flowering lilac bush. A withered lilac bush would not have horrified him, because he was aware that sooner or later the blooming bush would become a withered bush which is merely an expression of the natural rhythm of life. But the decayed state of the man could not be harmonized with the flowering nature around him. The pilot's recoil reflected his sense that this dead soldier was something contrary to life as God the Creator had planned it. The feeling came over him that the death of man is an unnatural thing. "And this young flier with his shock of horror," observes Thielicke, "was certainly nearer to the world of the New Testament and its message than the people who are always driveling about the 'naturalness' of human death." [4]

Heidegger is correct in his assertion that from Paul to Calvin Christian theology has been written in "the consciousness of death." According to the New Testament teaching, death is the result of sin and is the last enemy to be conquered. The apostle Paul declared: "The wages of sin is death" (Rom. 6:23). "The sting of death is sin" (1 Cor. 15:56). "Therefore as sin came into the world through one man and death through sin, and so death spread to all men because all men sinned" (Rom. 5:12). "The last enemy to be destroyed is death" (1 Cor. 15:26). Death is seen, then, from the biblical perspective not merely as a biological fact, but it is seen primarily as a moral fact.

Death is an enemy; it is not a part of order but disorder. Sin is the Christian way of explaining the reality of death. Sin is seen as man's rebellion against the source of his very being—God. This rebellion results in separation from God, outside of whom is only death. It results also in man's separation from his loved ones by death. This linking of death with sin seems to go against the grain of modern society and sounds like some ancient mythological way of speaking which should be forgotten and dismissed. Before you cast it aside, however, look first at what you may be surrendering. Let's see if we can determine where the biblical writers were heading with such a strange sounding doctrine.

"Death is so final," we often say, and the Christian faith teaches a finality about it that is even more threatening than some have been willing to accept. Many religions, especially the ancient Greek view of immortality, have at the center of their concept of death the idea that there is something within man, a divine spark or something akin to it, which never dies but continues after man's physical body dies. But this is not so in the Christian faith. The Old and New Testaments affirm strongly the unity of man—body, mind and spirit—and when man dies the destruction is total and complete.

Man, as understood in the biblical sense, does not have a soul which departs from his body at death, but man is a soul (Gen. 2:7). Many of the ancient Greeks despised the body and viewed man's body as a prison or a tomb which contained his soul. The body itself was seen as evil and the soul finally found release from its confinement at death. In contrast to this view, the New Testament focuses on the salvation of the whole man and not just his soul. When man dies, all of him dies, not just his body, and his salvation is concerned with the whole man and not just a part of him called a soul. The New Testament writers were aware that flesh and blood cannot inherit the kingdom of God, but they spoke of the resurrection of the body as the act of God who would recreate and glorify the body so the perishable was transformed into the imperishable.

Among some of the ancient Greek thinkers, the soul was depicted as a spark from God which had entered into the body of man, but the death of the body freed the soul so that it could be absorbed once again into God's being. But this absorption, however, meant the loss of personhood and individuality for man. The New Testament emphasis on the resurrection of the body is the biblical way of expressing the idea that the personality of man is not obliterated at death but that the individual personality of each believer survives death. This survival will be in the form of a glorified, transformed, spiritual body, which will be imperishable and incorruptible (1 Cor. 15:35-54; 2 Cor. 5:1-8).

Death is both a challenge and a threat to the total man. Like the child's jingle says:

> I had a little dog
> > His name was Rover,
> When he lived,
> > He lived on clover,
> When he died,
> > He died all over.

Some preachers have used the awesome finality of death as a means of persuading people to come to Jesus for redemption before it is "too late." Albert Schweitzer, in a sermon delivered at St. Nicolai's Church, noted that in the past it was considered Christian to use man's fear of death in order to frighten him into believing in eternal life. He tells about a famous chaplain in a French king's court who would point from his pulpit to the vaults where the nobility were buried along the wall of the royal chapel and describe how those who were now dead used to sit in the chapel, dressed in their finery, full of life and gaiety, and listened to his voice as those present were now doing. He then painted a gruesome picture, describing the past royalty as now buried, decaying, and rotting away. After this awful description, he believed his listeners were now ready to hear a sermon on repentance and eternal life.

"But what had he preached to them?" Schweitzer asked. "The sovereignty of death. Where there is terror and fear of death, there death reigns." [5] The Christian faith, however, does not want to propose "the sovereignty of death" but it declares that Christ died to "deliver all those who through fear of death were subject to lifelong bondage" (Heb. 2:15).

If man were able to solve the riddle about death, then all other questions would become secondary. In the biblical concept, death is not merely the last moment of life but it is "the last enemy to be destroyed" (1 Cor. 15:26). The New Testament answer to the mystery of death is a strange word—resurrection. Death, as a part of the total mystery of life, does not have the final word to say about man's existence; the ultimate word has been declared in the resurrection of Jesus Christ. The New Testament resounds with this sense of exultation, and nowhere is it more clearly evident than in 1 Corinthians 15. Listen to Paul as he shouts a victory cry:

> Death is swallowed up in victory.
> O death, where is thy victory?
> O death, where is thy sting?
> The sting of death is sin, and the
>   power of sin is the law.
> But thanks be to God, who gives us the
>   victory through our Lord Jesus Christ (1 Cor. 15:55-56).

"But wait a minute," modern man wants to say. "The word resurrection doesn't help much. Resurrection sounds offensive and unreal in this Space Age." Why does modern man assume he is any different in his reaction to this word than ancient man? Paul had the attention of the crowd of Athenians at Areopagus until he uttered the strange word, resurrection, and then most of them jeered and walked away. No, the ancient mind found the word as unpalatable as contemporary, urban man does. The Stoics insisted that man learned to face his death bravely as the natural biological conclusion to one's existence. The Epicureans laughed and said: "Live life to the fullest in this life, since there is nothing after death, no harm can come to you, then, eat, drink and be merry for tomorrow we die." Even the Hebrew mind, except for a few fleeting insights, noted in Psalms 16:8-11; 73:21-26; Job 19:24-27; Isaiah 26:19; and Daniel 12:2-3, conceived of life after death as only a shadowy sort of existence in Sheol.

A strong belief in life after death did not become a vital part of the Hebrew belief until during what is usually called the interbiblical period—that time between the last written document of the Old Testament and the New when the Jewish nation came greatly under the influence of Persian philosophy. To the Greek mind the notion of resurrection was appalling; man had an immortal soul, and at the time of his death his divine soul flew from the body which had been its prison to give it full release to return to heaven. So ancient thoughts about death and the possibility of life beyond it closely parallel the pattern of secular, urban man: scepticism, agnosticism, unbelief, stoic acceptance, death as a natural process, and a belief by some few in the immortality of the soul.

Death is a mystery, yes, but so is resurrection. But this latter mystery is set forth by the church to answer the former. The problem of death is central to the Christian faith, because the awesome reality and dimension of sin are taken with genuine seriousness. Adam, every man, has fallen; he has chosen the way of death—the path of sin—estrangement from God, his fellowman, and even his authentic self. The New Testament posits incarnation, cross, redemption, atonement, salvation, and resurrection to remove the barriers of sin, evil, fragmentation, lostness, and death. Sin is costly; it results in death. The New Testament "good news," the gospel, lifts up the cross-resurrection as God's answer to the tragedy of sin-death.

Perhaps our difficulty in understanding the New Testament's ringing assurance in the resurrection is that we have not taken seriously enough the terrible nature of sin. Paul reminded the Corinthian church about the nature of the gospel he first preached to them: "For I delivered to you as of first importance what I also received, that Christ died for our sins . . . that he was buried, that he was raised on the third day" (1 Cor. 15:3-4). Again, Paul declared forcefully:

For if we have been united with him in a death like his, we shall certainly be united with him in a resurrection like his. We know that our old self was crucified with him so that the sinful body might be destroyed, and we might no longer be enslaved to sin. For he who has died is freed from sin. But if we have died with Christ, we believe that we shall also live with him. For we know that Christ being raised from the dead will never die again; death no longer has dominion over him. The death he died he died to sin, once for all, but the life he lives he lives to God. So you also must consider yourself dead to sin and alive to God in Christ Jesus (Rom. 6:5-11).

"For whatever is truly wondrous and fearful in man, never yet was put into words or books," wrote Herman Melville. "And the drawing near of Death, which alike levels all, alike impresses all with a last revelation, which only an author from the dead could adequately tell." Isn't this the claim of the church? One from the dead has returned to share with us his revelation, his victory—Jesus Christ, the living Lord. According to the New Testament the foundation stone upon which the Christian church is built is the resurrection of Jesus Christ.

Let us focus on the significance which the resurrection of Jesus has for our faith and the light it may shed on the mystery of death. The New Testament discussion of the resurrection of Jesus revolves around at least three great affirmations about Christ, God, and man.

Death and the Resurrection of Jesus

"Christianity stands or falls with the reality of the raising of Jesus from the dead by God," so declares contemporary theologian

Jurgen Moltmann. "In the New Testament there is no faith that does not start *a priori* with the resurrection of Jesus." [6] "In the resurrection of Jesus," another contemporary theologian, Wolfhart Pannenberg, states: "We therefore have to do with the sustaining foundation of the Christian faith. If this collapses, so does everything else which the Christian faith acknowledges." [7]

The apostle Paul pointed in the same direction when he argued: "If Christ has not been raised, your faith is still futile and you are still in your sins" (1 Cor. 15:17). The resurrection was not a secondary or debatable matter with Paul; if it fell, the whole house of faith collapsed with it; if it proved false, nothing else mattered. It was the one essential truth on which, he believed, all the rest of the faith depended—salvation, forgiveness, reconciliation, and hope for life beyond the grave.

Paul, along with the other writers of the New Testament, was aware that what Jesus is stands for more than what he said. Paul had the emphasis in the right place when he spoke of the risen Christ and not the Sermon on the Mount. The ethical and moral teachings of Jesus are important and should not be minimized, but the vitality of all his teachings take on a new dimension in light of the resurrection. He died as he had taught men to live, self-sacrificially; however, without the resurrection the cross would have marked the tragic end to the life of a good and wise young teacher. The resurrection is a confirmation of the incarnation, "that God was in Christ reconciling the world unto himself."

Resurrection affirms that Jesus was who he said he was; that what he said was from one who had the authority to say it, and that, in approval of a life lived and laid down for the sin of man, God raised Jesus up. "A Christian faith that is not resurrection faith," Moltmann says, "can therefore be called neither Christian nor faith. It is the knowledge of the risen Lord and the confession to him who raised him that form the basis on which the memory of the life, work, sufferings and death of Jesus is kept alive and presented in the gospels." [8]

Many today are still living on the wrong side of the Easter event. They are caught in the middle between Friday and Easter

Sunday. They have stopped after the crucifixion and remained on Saturday in despair. They have become Saturday's children. Saturday's child is caught between the Friday of death and the Sunday of resurrection. He has not moved to the dawn of hope, so he still dwells in despair, fear, meaninglessness, and defeat.

Can you imagine what that Saturday must have been like to the disciples of Jesus after his horrible crucifixion? Look and listen for a moment to the disciples as they may have gathered together in the upper room. Their faces are drawn and saddened by the events; their eyes are darkened from want of sleep; despair fills their hearts and minds. The vision of the messianic kingdom seems defeated, Peter decides to return to his old job of fishing. Where would the others go? Could Matthew collect taxes again? What could they do now? The blush of shame is still felt in the faces of some. Peter can never forget his denial of his Lord in the courtyard, "I never knew him." Disciples who said they were fortified to "drink his cup" and would never forsake him had fled to safety when danger appeared, only the women and John stayed near the cross. Fear also filled their eyes. The door was bolted shut; they were afraid that the Roman or religious authorities who had put Jesus to death might be looking for them now.

There they huddled on Saturday, hearts broken with despair, minds tormented with fright, bodies weary from sleepless exhaustion, spirits tormented with defeat and their dreams shattered. They were Saturday's children—with a long way to go—but on Sunday morning the dawn of a new hope broke upon them—the resurrection of Jesus. They had not looked for it; had not expected it; could hardly believe it. But once the light of that resurrection morning began to shatter the darkness of their despair, a faith, joy, and hope unfolded which turned defeat to victory, tears to laughter, sadness to joy, tragedy to hope, despair to celebration, cowardliness to courage, faithlessness to commitment, and disciples to apostles. An unbelievable event had taken place.

The resurrection is a unique event as an act of God which transcends history, and it summons man to a radical commitment of faith to a living Lord. "If you confess with your lips that Jesus is Lord and believe in your heart that God raised him from the dead, you will be saved" (Rom. 10:9).

We sometimes too quickly or too easily forget the manner in which Christ himself faced the prospect of his own death. "When they reached a place called Gethsemane, he said to his disciples, 'Sit here while I pray.' And he took Peter and James and John with him. Horror and dismay came over him, and he said to them, 'My heart is ready to break with grief; stop here, and stay awake.' Then he went forward a little, threw himself on the ground, and prayed that, if it were possible, this hour might pass him by" (Mark 14:32-35, NEB). Some have dismissed Jesus' fear of death as merely the awesome spiritual agony he knew he had to face, but others have observed in his response the normal reaction that all humanity senses in the realization of approaching death. His peace came later as he emerged from Gethsemane armed with a sense of God's will and grace.

As Jesus faced the dark enigma of death, he walked as we walk by faith—with the same feelings, frustrations, hopes, fears and emotions—but in his faith he moved with a vital awareness of the trustworthiness, reliability and presence of God. Marney is right; Jesus "faithed" his way through death just as we must do, and he had no "life-back-guarantee," but he "bet his life" on the Father he served.

In Jesus Christ we see Adam, man, as he was meant to be—not partial, not fragmented, not incomplete but whole, full, complete man. "God cuts through the strands of human history in an incarnation, an enfleshing," Marney says, "to make a demonstration of what man is like when he is completed. God's idea, his realized demonstration, is Jesus Christ, Redeemer, Son of God, *monogones* (only one of its kind), who invades history as its Master and finished product not only to demonstrate but to make completion possible." [9] As the new Adam, Jesus Christ, who has been raised from the dead, then becomes "the first fruits of those who have fallen asleep" (1 Cor. 15:20). He is also "the faithful witness, the firstborn of the dead" (Rev. 1:5). The Christian has hope in the face of death because he puts his trust in the same power which brought life to him in the beginning, Jesus Christ.

Our hope for life after death is based on the resurrection of Jesus Christ from the dead. Any continuity for life after death is grounded in a power outside ourselves, the power of God himself who alone is able to raise the dead. "If Christ has not been raised," Paul asserts, "your faith is futile and you are still in your sins" (1 Cor. 15:17). But our faith is: "because he lives, we shall live also." "I am the resurrection and the life; he who believes in me, though he die, yet shall he live, and whoever lives and believes in me shall never die" (John 11:25).

Death and the Nature of God

The "why's" surrounding death will not cease their relentless inquiry easily. For many they reach all the way into the very presence of God. Some simply say softly, "I'll ask God one day and he'll explain all." Others will have none of it. They cry out bitterly: "If he cares; if he is so loving, why did she die?—I just do not understand it!" Some are bold enough to assert that man's death raises a moral question directed at the very nature of God himself. "Fundamentally man's death appears to indict the Creator," says New Testament scholar, Leander E. Keck, "for it raises the question, How did it happen that the undying Creator made life subject to death?" [10]

This question lifts out the central problem—death poses questions about the very integrity of God himself. But the New Testament pushes the pointer around the other way and focuses the blame not on God but man. Some would like to dismiss the Genesis story of the Fall as mere ancient mythology, but no matter how you size up the account, Adam—every man—rebels from God's fellowship by his free choice, not by God's rejection. Man turns from God, not God from man. The conclusion is something we may not like, but it is unavoidable—the New Testament links death with man's sin. Our sin, we must admit, is real. Few have expressed it as well as the late theologian Paul Tillich:

Thus, the state of our whole life is estrangement from others and ourselves, because we are estranged from the Ground of our being, because we are estranged from the origin and aim of our life. And we do not know where we have come from, or where we are going. We are separated from the mystery, the depth, and the greatness of our existence. We hear the voice of that depth; but our ears are closed. We feel that something radical, total, and unconditioned is demanded of us; but we rebel against it, try to escape its urgency, and will not accept its promise.[11]

Without question, man's knowledge of his own certain demise is entangled with an understanding of the character of God. That should not cause despair; it is the ground for confident hope. In the middle of an argument with the religious sect called the Sadducees who did not believe in the resurrection of the dead, Jesus pointed them to the Pentateuch, the only section of the Old Testament Scriptures which they accepted as authentic. There he confronted them with their own Scriptures. "And as for the dead being raised, have you not read in the book of Moses, in the passage about the bush, how God said to him, 'I am the God of Abraham, and the God of Isaac, and the God of Jacob'? He is not God of the dead, but of the living; you are quite wrong" (Mark 12:26-27). What has that got to do with resurrection? Everything! The implication and declaration of Jesus is that Abraham, Isaac, and Jacob are still living in a vital relationship to God—even death has not severed the tie which bound them to him.

Here, then, is the real lesson about the integrity and character of the God of the universe: he does not blow out the personality of man as if it were a dime-store candle; he has not placed in our hearts a quest for the eternal to turn around and snatch it from our grasp; he has not created us in his image whimsically to toss us aside as valueless; he has not planted this restlessness within us to extinguish it without a sense of fulfillment. As Jesus told the Sadducees, we do not know the Scriptures nor the power of God.

The nature and character of God are evidences of the assurance we can have that God will not cast aside his creation but will sustain a vital relationship with it. What God has started with man, he will finish. Man is yet incomplete but God is pulling us toward completion. We are not yet—as much as—what we can be—long to be—hope to be—should be—can be—but it is his power which will enable us to become. When God looked upon his whole creation, even man or maybe especially man, God did not say that it was perfect or complete; "And God saw everything that he had made and behold, it was very good" (Gen. 1:31).

Paul was willing to push the mystery beyond man to nature itself. It, too, is incomplete, not fulfilled. Why is there so much tragedy even within nature's "angry red claw"? Do the little fish and small animals exist only to be devoured by the larger creatures? "A veil of sadness is spread over all nature," Schelling said, "a deep unappeasable melancholy over all life." Nature's tragedy is linked with man's, Paul was bold to assert:

For the creation waits with eager longing for the revealing of the sons of God; for the creation was subjected to futility, not of its own will but by the will of him who subjected it in hope; because the creation itself will be set free from its bondage to decay and obtain the glorious liberty of the children of God. We know that the whole creation has been groaning in travail together until now; and not only the creation, but we ourselves, who have the first fruits of the Spirit, groan inwardly as we wait for adoption as sons, the redemption of our bodies (Rom. 8:19-23).

Man is apart from nature and yet is a part *of* nature. Man and nature are tied together in a web of life. As man moves toward atonement with God, so the natural order seeks its at-one-ment. There is a solidarity not only which man shares with all humanity but which he bears with all living things. The ecologists have warned man what his pollution and wasteful style of life have already unleashed upon the world. Lewis Mumford stated man's dilemma when he wrote: "Though he is now the dominant species, his fate is still bound up with the prosperity of all forms of life." [12] Natural as well as moral laws of the universe have

been violated by man and the redemptive process is concerned
not only with man but with all creation which is itself moving
toward fulfillment. "The tragedy of nature," Tillich observes, "is
bound to the tragedy of man, as the salvation of nature is dependent on the salvation of man." [13] Tied together by a chord that
will not fully free one without the other, man and nature move
toward the completeness which God has created them to have.

I have to confess that I cannot understand very clearly the
frightful hold sin has on man and the world nor the way God's
power shatters its grip and sets us free. It's tough trying to understand talk about redemption of man, much less nature, but I am
also struck by the limited and partial nature of any knowledge
which I might have.

My small five-year-old son is not able yet to grasp the meaning
of many multi-syllable words I might be able to read, but that
does not lessen my love for him nor my intention of guiding him
into deeper knowledge. His limited knowledge does not mean
that I cannot have a meaningful relationship with him which will
deepen and enrich our love, compassion, and understanding. Just
because his knowledge is limited and his perspective is childish
does not mean that he cannot know me, love me, and respond
to me. He can and does. My knowledge of God, from his perspective, in fact from any, must seem so childish, immature, primitive,
limited, narrow, and confining, but this does not mean that I
cannot have some knowledge and live and act on the basis of
the partial knowledge of God which I do have. I am certain that
as the Father, he is seeking to guide me into deep insights.

Our knowledge of God is limited but that we can know him,
at least partially, is a Christian certainty. Once when a traveler
became lost in the hills of Tennessee, he stopped at a small
crossroads store and asked an old gentleman where Knoxville was.
"I don't know, Mister," the old man replied, "where Knoxville
is, 'cause I've never been there, but there's the road to it." Our
knowledge of God, like the old man's knowledge of Knoxville,
may be limited and partial, but we know the way. Jesus Christ,
himself, has made the way clear and now we seek to walk in

it. We have become "men of the way."

Death and the Nature of Man

The question of the psalmist is echoed through the centuries. "What is man, that thou art mindful of him?" (Ps. 8:4) Who and what is this man-woman creature? He is an enigma. He loves and hates; he is kind and cruel; he is brave and cowardly; he is understanding and judgmental; he is compassionate and mean. With one hand man reaches out to lift up a fallen companion; the other hand pulls a trigger to take a life. A strong arm helps a weary traveler; the other pulls a lever to knock down a building. With strong legs man scales a mountain or blocks the path of another man moving toward freedom. With his mind man can focus his attention to think the thoughts of God after him or plan diabolical ways of destroying the human race. Who is man; he is a menagerie. He wants to be Prometheus, Superman—to be a god. He wants to rule the land, the sea, and the air. His greatest sin is his "God almightyness."

There is an inseparable link between sin and death, so that death follows from sin. According to Emil Brunner:

Sin is not merely moral evil, but the rebellion of the creature against the Creator. When man as sinner denies his dependence on God and turns it into independence, he is severed from God the original source of all life; his guilt stands between the living God and himself as he actually is. Then the creature destroys the rest of its own life, its fellowship with God.[14]

In Jesus Christ we see the New Adam—man as he should be—related fully to the Source of life. "For there is one God, and there is one mediator between God and men, the man Christ Jesus" (1 Tim. 2:5). I like Frank Stagg's way of understanding the title of mediator as applied to Jesus Christ. He sees mediator as meaning more than someone who is between God and man. "Jesus came *to overcome the betweenness* between God and man."[15] In Jesus Christ we are able to have a deeper look into the nature of both God and man.

Some people have been content to depict man as an animal and no more. Others see man as a complicated machine, while another describes man as an accident of fate whose life is without purpose or meaning. On the other hand, the biblical picture of man presents him as a creature who has been created in the image of God (Gen. 1:26-27; 1 Cor. 11:7). The creation of the image of God within man was God's way of endowing man with some measure of his own personal nature. Because man has been created in the image of God, it is possible for him to have communion with God. This fact indicates the eternal significance which God has given to human personality.

"Whatever the doubtful phrase, 'the image of God,' may mean," states H. Wheeler Robinson, "it is certainly intended to recognize man's unique relation to God, and his supremacy over the animal world." [16] God's revealing love of himself was not given to inanimate rocks and water but to man; it is person to person. Man is what he is because God created him different from the dust of the ground, animals, or plants; he was created to have fellowship with God. God has given to man the gift of self-conscious reason, and this is distinctive of man alone of all of creation. Man shares in the nature of God by God's creative act.

Man's rebellion against God is taken very seriously by God. The "wages of sin is death," but God loves man too much not to seek restoration. The coming of the "Word . . . made flesh" shows the supreme worth God maintains for his creation. God continually wants to preserve the unique personality of man both in this life and the life after death. If man were not significant to God, the incarnation would not have happened in the first place. Maybe this is the reason some people still reject the incarnation today; their opinion of man is too low—he is not worth redeeming.

God's grace and love in Jesus Christ reveal the lengths to which he will go to bring man back into his fellowship. For this reason, it seems impossible to accept talk of the annihilation and extinction of human personality at death as having any plausible grounds on which to stand. Many contemporary writers have given way to a spirit of hopelessness which has begun to overwhelm the outlook of man. John Baillie maintains, however, that the Christian does have hope and a hope not only in his present existence but in the life to come after death. The Christian's hope is based on his personal knowledge of the eternal God and is rooted in man's continuous religious fellowship with the eternal God. Man's hope of eternal life issues out of his awareness that he can have knowledge of God in communion with him. The only unanswerable argument for life after death, Baillie believes, is realized in the fact that God is the God of individuals who can enter into fellowship with him. Baillie sets forth what he calls a "logic of hope." "If the individual can commune with God, then he must matter to God; and if he matters to God, he must share God's eternity." [17] The Christian hope of eternal life is grounded in man's fellowship with God.

Eternal Life as Present and Future

Many of us have difficulty understanding the concept of resurrection for the Christian because it seems to suggest both that it is something to be realized in the distant future and that it is also a present possession of the believer. One needs to be honest and admit that the New Testament contains descriptions of both viewpoints. The concept of a future consummation is depicted in 1 Thessalonians 4 and 1 Corinthians 15:52-58, along with other passages, where Paul says that those who are dead will be awakened at the return of Christ with a cry from the archangel and the sound of the trumpet of God. Romans 8 speaks even of a future cosmic redemption of both man and nature.

At the same time Paul says that he was eager to "depart and be with Christ" (Phil. 1:23) at the time of death and that "the old had already passed away and that the new had already come and that everyone in Christ was already a new creation" (2 Cor. 5:17). Many other places could be suggested to show the varying descriptions of what the resurrected life is to be like. Is there any way to reconcile the two? Can resurrection be both present and future?

Stagg has looked at this apparent contradiction and concluded: "What appears to be a time interval to us who are bound by time may be no interval at all to God or to those who through death have entered into eternity with him. The resurrection which is future to those within time may be present reality to those who have died and who are now with the Lord in a bodily state." [18] Brunner has expressed it well. "The date of death differs for each man for the day of death belongs to this world. Our day of resurrection is the same for all and yet is not separated from the day of death by intervals of centuries for these time-intervals are here not there in the presence of God, where 'a thousand years are as a day.'" [19] In some sense God, to whom one day is "as a thousand years, and a thousand years as one day" (2 Pet. 3:8), transcends time and relates his eternal life for man both as a present possession and a future reality.

Eternal life for the Christian is not merely something which begins when he dies but is a dimension of existence in which he begins here and now. The resurrection of Jesus Christ marks the coming of the new age, and now the church proclaims that through Christ's death and resurrection forgiveness of sin and new life are available to men of faith. The message, however, is that the new life is a present possession of the believer which begins with his trust. "And this is eternal life, that they know thee the only true God, and Jesus Christ whom thou hast sent" (John 17:3. See also 2 Cor. 4:10-11; 1 John 4:9).

The Christian faith notes the awesome seriousness of death and does not see man as having some part, or spark, or soul, or spirit that can depart from his body without death touching it. Man is a unit; and a whole person, and he does not possess a soul; he is a soul. When he dies biologically he dies totally, and he is then raised by God as a "spiritual body," transformed, imperishable, glorified, and with power, to be like the last Adam, Christ, his Lord (1 Cor. 15:44-57). The New Testament does not maintain that we will have the same physical body, but like a grain of wheat, Paul says, it will be changed, but we will not lose our own identity or uniqueness (Phil. 3:21; Acts 17:31).

The New Testament, especially the Gospel of John, does not make a distinction between the time of this world and the time of the realm where one lives after death. In fact, John's Gospel states that eternal life is a present possession of the Christian; it transforms the present and makes one aware of living in eternity now. Through Christ even the time barrier has been overcome. To know God through his Son is to possess eternal life now.

The Greek word for eternal is not concerned so much with length of life but with the quality of life. Eternal life is the life of God and through an intimate, personal relationship which Christ has made available, man can participate here and now in the eternal life of God. Even death itself cannot destroy this relationship. "Truly, truly, I say to you, he who believes has eternal life" (John 6:47). God's time is eternity and he is the only one "from everlasting to everlasting" (Ps. 90:2); "the same yesterday and today and for ever" (Heb. 13:8); He is the "Alpha and Omega, . . . which is, . . . and which is to come, the Almighty" (Rev. 1:8, KJV). The one who has initiated the "new creation" is the one the Scriptures declare was with God "in the beginning" (John 1:1). The Lord over time has given men who live in time an opportunity to share in eternity through fellowship with him. God's love has reached out to man before the "foundation of the world" (John 17:24; Rev. 13:8). God's eternal love is boundless, and it stretches back beyond history and forward into the fulfillment of time.

Many methods have been used to try to peer behind the veil of death to see if anything is there. In their quest, men have attempted to read the stars, tea leaves, palms, crystal balls, and cards; they have listened to mediums who allegedly talk with the dead; some have even dreamed of "time machines" which would carry a person into the future and beyond. Few have found much lasting satisfaction through these paths. For many, life seems to be heading for a dead-end street. The grave seems to pronounce a final word of defeat to the meaning and purpose of life. The New Testament, however, is bold to assert that the decisive victory over sin and death has already been won through the life, death, and resurrection of Jesus Christ. "D day" has already come! The war may continue for some time yet, but the decisive battle has already been accomplished through Christ's victory over the grave.

The last book in the Bible relates the victory cry as the seer of Patmos records his vision of the living Christ. "Behold I am alive for evermore, and I have the keys of Death and Hades" (Rev. 1:18). The Christian hope rings through the centuries in the words of Jesus to Martha: "I am the resurrection and the life; he who believes in me, though he die, yet shall he live, and whoever lives and believes in me shall never die" (John 11:25-26).

The complete mystery of death is never fully removed, but the Christian seeks to meet it as Lord Balfour did when he closed his eyes in death and whispered, "This is going to be a great experience." Life is a great gift; we rejoice in it and want to use this great gift to the fullest of our capacity. We are reminded, however, by Schweitzer's interpretation of the apostle Paul that we know that this world is "a house sold for the breaking up" and so we will live in it with care; but we will not invest our entire holdings in it. A man can die, or he can die in Jesus Christ. Man can die as only a biological creature, or he can die as a child of nature and a child of God. At the moment of death, we are absolutely dependent upon faith. At this critical moment, all else fails us—wealth, pride, prestige, power, influence, friends. The only available resource for us is faith in God. Here in this moment, as in no other, we must acknowledge an absolute dependence on the power of God—our power is totally diminished—we are wholly dependent on the Holy One.

The Christian approaches death with the awareness that "the last enemy to be destroyed is death." Death is not man's "natural" end but is an enemy of God and stands in opposition to God's ultimate will. "Death is the peak of all that is contrary to God in the world, the last *enemy*," says Karl Barth, "thus not the natural lot of man, not an unalterable divine dispensation." [20] But Jesus Christ has already won the battle against death and and so Paul can shout: "Thanks be to God, who gives us the victory through our Lord Jesus Christ" (1 Cor. 15:57). Death for the Christian becomes a transitional path from this life to the next; it is not a dead-end street but a thoroughfare that leads into another dimension of living. "Death is no more the dark door that shuts forever behind man," Brunner says, "but the opened door through which he enters into true life." [21]

Imagine how a baby might try to philosophize if he were able to contemplate another kind of life outside his mother's womb. What could he use as a base from which to speculate or surmise? How could he understand life free from surrounding liquid? What does he know of light, or breath, or food, or eating? What does he know of choices, companionship, friends, work, art, reading? Is it not possible that to the infant the birth process is to him a crisis which is a sort of "death" as he leaves his safe, comfortable, secure world where his every need had been met? A new and marvelous world awaits him; he has no resources to imagine what it will be like—and how wonderfully different from his other world. Death for the Christian is a "birthing" from the physical world to the spiritual realm. How can we possibly describe it; words fail us. "What no eye has seen, nor ear heard, nor the heart of man conceived, what God has prepared for those who love him" (1 Cor. 2:9).

The bandages were slowly being cut away from the eyes of the ten-year-old boy. He had been blind since birth. His parents waited, breathlessly hoping that he would now be able to see. The surgeon turned the boy's head toward the window and asked him to open his eyes slowly. At first the light was blinding but then his eyes began to focus on some flowers outside the window and the young lad shouted: "But why didn't you tell me it was so beautiful?" His father's only reply was, "We tried to, son! We tried to." When man opens his eyes after the "birthing" from the physical to the spiritual realm and glimpses the beauty and wonder of eternity, will he not also ask, "But why didn't you tell me it was so beautiful?" Our Lord will say, "I tried to!"

6

A Teacher Looks at Death

The problem of death and the right to die is more than a topic for verbal discussion. It is an experience. There are some persons we know who are confronting death in an immediate way, and some in these situations are living with the moral question of the right to die. In their experiences they provide the real substance for the question of death and the right to die.

I was greatly interested to learn a few years ago that certain students in my ethics class had experienced a moral conflict in this area. When I began teaching at Virginia Intermont College, one of my duties was to teach a course in ethics. Since I had spent some four years of graduate work concentrating on ethical issues, I looked forward to the opportunity to share my pearls of wisdom with bright and inquiring college students. After all, hadn't I kept up with such moral problems as war and violence, the sexual revolution, and civil rights? Wouldn't students become totally immersed in an in-depth study of such timely matters? They did not! Oh, they were interested but not really "turned-on." This may have been due to what appears to be a shift of focus of interest on the college campuses.

An open, class discussion quickly brought out what appeared to be the key ethical issue for that semester: death and the right to die. (Whether this topic is the main ethical concern for all student populations is yet to be determined.) One student asked:

"My grandmother is eighty-seven and wants to die; what do I say when she insists on talking with me about whether it is right to think about killing herself? My parents think it's morbid."

Another student said, "My father's friend was a terminal cancer patient; the methods used to keep him alive left the friend unconscious for the last six weeks of his life. The financial and mental strain on his family was so intense that my father wondered if they shouldn't have let the man die earlier . . . and yet my father felt guilty for even thinking such a thought."

Still another confided, "When my brother was killed in an accident, my family was so torn up that no one would talk to me about his death. I felt and still feel that this was wrong. We should have talked and cried together."

At this point the ethics class came alive. Almost all of the students had experienced the phenomenon of conflict in death situations. And, in one way or another, each raised basic moral questions about life and death. Do I, does anyone, have the right to die? Does a family have the right to tell a physician to stop treatment on a relative who is a patient? Where do family rights and responsibilities begin and end in relation to a dying member, and vice versa? Should the family feel obligated to discuss and confront death together?

What follows is a general summary of some of the observations made by the ethics class.

The right to live and die. The class's initial observation was that the primary human right was the right to life. But, this right was interpreted to mean, "the right to a certain quality of life." The problem then became that of determining what "quality of life" meant. The class's solution was found in the term "dignity": every person had the right to live life with dignity . . . and it was assumed that all knew what dignity meant. (It seems to me that such a term is best defined by illustrating "a violation" of human dignity. For example, the class agreed that to keep a person alive in a vegetable state was a violation of that person's right to dignity and life.) This interpretation of the right to life is an important one, because it implied that if a certain quality of life were not maintained (or maintainable) one might indeed have *a right* to die. Indeed, this was the class's conclusion: There may be instances in which an individual (a terminal patient, for example) is forced to assume a life without dignity, and therefore, the individual has the right to claim a life with dignity through choosing to die.

But, what does it mean to have the right to die with dignity? Somewhat paradoxically, the class seemed to believe that it meant that one has "the right to live the death experience." The right to life and the right to death were the same thing. From this perspective, then, death was not viewed as "the end of it all"; rather, death was a part of life. Death remained "death" but it also meant something like fulfillment, or "a necessary and important event to be prepared for and experienced." Therefore, a terminally ill patient had the right to refuse medication if such aid would, in the patient's (and the family's) view, take away from the patient's coherent experience of life's death process.

Of course, there were numerous contradictions in the class discussions. Pain, for example, a definite part of many death experiences, was to be avoided. Medical aid for pain was not viewed to be antithetical to the life's death process, while drugs which simply prolonged life were. Be that as it may, the significant, moral conclusion was that the right to life involved the right to experience the death process with dignity. The human person had the right to live life and "death as a part of life" with dignity.

Death and the family. The next stage of class discussion shifted to family responsibilities. Specifically, the class concluded that the subject of death "ought" to be discussed by the family.

From one angle it was argued that the privilege to discuss not only ideas and theories (freedom of speech) but also to share intimate fears and anxieties was an essential *right* of human dignity related to the specific life process of mental and physical health and human fulfillment. Every person had the right to express his innermost feelings with "appropriate" people at "appropriate" times.

The conditional term "appropriate" was added to restrict a

person from thinking that he had the right to share innermost feelings with "just anyone" and at "just anytime." However, there were "appropriate people" with whom one had "the right" to discuss his innermost feeling concerning death.

This area of discussion was initially directed by that person whose family had rejected her attempt to discuss her brother's death: "It was too horrible to discuss!" the family said. The class response to this situation was that the family was wrong, that an injustice had been done. But more important was the further discussion which led to the conclusion that every family "ought" to deal directly and indirectly with the problem of death. The family was generally conceived as the most intimate and personal circle of human relationships. By its very nature as an institution "it" was obligated to nurture its members toward human maturity. For a family to neglect the open confrontation with any life issue was a violation of a primary responsibility which it held.

Directly and indirectly, the class accepted certain persons outside the family as "appropriate persons" with whom death could be discussed. Close friends were particularly appropriate, as were ministers and counselors (in varying degrees). In general the minister and counselor were accepted as "appropriate" because they were viewed as specialists. Most students knew their home-church minister and valued his friendship, thus making an open discussion of death with him fairly comfortable. The counselor was viewed more questionably, perhaps because he was seen as "too professional." As one student put it, "I hope I never get so messed up that I have to go to a counselor!" Nevertheless, all saw the minister's and the counselor's experience with death as something of a source and guide for personal understanding. Further, the minister and counselor had the acceptable roles of one-to-one counseling and, equally important, family and/or group counseling. This latter role was significant because it was a means, if not the means, whereby the students saw the family having the opportunity to confront death indirectly. In short, the minister and counselor were sources for family education.

The ethics class personalized for me many questions related

to death and the right to die. I find myself in almost complete agreement on the point of the family's responsibility to confront death and the point that death should be viewed as *one* important experience to be confronted in life's process. Psychologically it seems that the more abundant life is lived when we struggle with and confront our experiences, and that in the sometimes feared encounter ironically "we find ourselves free to be."

But this confrontation with death takes on a new dimension when the shift is made from the event of death to the idea of people choosing to die. The matter becomes more complex when one moves from the terminal patient's decision to cease medication and an elderly person's decision "to drink the hemlock."

In part, my Christian background is boggling my mind. I am aware, for example, that the early Christian community viewed suicide as a sin and that one tendency today is to do the same. "The person who contemplates or commits suicide," one minister said, "is simply running from the challenges in life that our Lord put before him . . . he is shirking his responsibilities to loved ones, to church, to community, to God! He is the worst of sinners." Of course, this opinion is modified by many. Certain psychologists of Christian persuasion, for example, see the problem of suicide more in terms of mental illness than sin. This view too, however, is primarily a negative response, suicide being the result of, for example, depression.

Can voluntary death be viewed more positively? In the case of the terminally ill patient who chooses to cease medication, the response can be affirmative. Such a decision *can be* an affirmation of faith. It can be a joyous thanksgiving for life and an adventurous step toward the reunion with God. In such instances it might well be agreed that to prolong life is demonstration of a lack of faith.

The case of the elderly person is more problematic. Yet, one *could* argue from an I-Thou stance that an elderly person is not avoiding the responsibility of the life that God has given them; rather, this person might well be affirming its fulfillment. It seems somewhat questionable to argue that God gives to certain elderly persons the responsibility to be senile or the responsibility to experience various degrees of physical complications related to age. Indeed, the longing of some to drink the hemlock may be in itself the voice of *The* Thou.

Dare we condone voluntary death to the terminally ill? Dare we step further and condone voluntary death to the aged? If asked by a brother to walk with him on this pilgrimage as far as we can go, dare we refuse? Dare we feel guilty for accepting the invitation and for demanding that our brother's wishes be granted? These moments are for God and for those fortunates who struggle and then let go to confront the Thou.

Dr. Tuck: You mentioned that the topic "Death and the Right to Die" was one of many topics which you discussed in your ethics course. Do you think it might be good if some of our schools offered a whole course in this area, dealing with death from many different viewpoints? Would this be morbid or helpful?

Dr. Lee: I am aware of some experiments in this area. What this experimenting did was to let people *see* death. The students worked in a mortuary for awhile, worked for physicians, and worked in emergency rooms. They learned enough about counseling to work with counselors in hospital situations. The overwhelming student response was that it was a liberating experience. If anything you teach can be liberating to the student, then you have achieved excellence in providing an environment in which education can (and did) take place. If death is a problem that all persons confront (and I believe it is), then it seems most worthwhile to deal with the issue in any educational institution. I am very much in favor of expanding the time to deal with the issue . . . even a year's course.

Dr. Tuck: Would you say from your experience with the students that at the conclusion of the course they were better prepared to face death?

Dr. Lee: Very much so. It was interesting, however, that there was an almost total rejection of the idea that pain could be a meaningful part of death. They could face death, but not painful death. We must remember, however, that for many of them it was the first time they had ever really talked about death. I did get the impression that for most of them death—even their own death—was no longer a "horrible thing." Many even spoke of it in terms of a good and positive experience.

DR. TUCK: I realize that this next question is very broad, but why do you think it is so difficult for people, students included, to talk about death?

DR. LEE: I will have to answer this question from a personal and religious perspective. I think the idea that death is the end of it all is the predominant attitude among people. And, from this perspective comes the fear of the end—the dreaded event that takes away whatever little there is in life. From the perspective of my faith, however, I think I am coming more and more to see death as simply a transition stage, something that is going to be a liberation of some sort. Now I don't know how bravely I am going to be able to confront my own death, but I don't think I fear death at all. The initial problem the students had in talking about death seemed to me to stem from the basic attitude that "death is the end of it all." They just don't look forward to it and they don't want to talk about it.

DR. TUCK: What I hear you saying is that without some sort of religious foundation death is seen as a final event.

DR. LEE: Yes. But let me add that for some who have no religious faith, the final event is not necessarily something to be feared. Rather it is a sort of grand finale in experience. Some of the students in the class, for example, professed no religious faith and yet claimed that they had come to view death in a very positive way. But for me, death is very closely tied to my religious convictions.

DR. TUCK: You mentioned the desire of the students to talk to individual members of their family about this kind of question. How do you think we can get families to talk more to each other about the possibility of their own death or the death of others, and what should they do in the light of it?

DR. LEE: In evaluating my own family, I think one of the

hang-ups is going to be that it is a terrific risk to get in a situation where you just let go completely and mourn and weep together. To my knowledge our society isn't really very big on getting together and doing things like that. A family has to commit itself to discuss any issue that it deems important to the welfare of the family. If the family decides that death is important, then it simply has to make the leap to say that this issue will be discussed. On the other hand, I think you can do things like we're doing in church . . . we're actually taking the risk to talk about death and dying! But initially, it's going to take a tremendous risk and a tremendous leap on the part of each family to commit itself to be open, to let go and talk. I think this is the crux of the matter.

DR. TUCK: We want to give others an opportunity to raise some questions.

QUESTION: I've got two questions. When you first started, you said something about a person on a machine being a vegetable— are you saying that you think it's right for a person to continue to live on a machine when the people around him know that he is going to be a vegetable for the rest of his life?

DR. LEE: The class decided that it was immoral to keep such a person alive. I'm not totally aware of the medical conflict here, but I think many physicians would maintain that once a machine or something of this sort is turned on (like a kidney machine or a heart machine) it's a real issue whether you can turn that machine off. And I do know of some spectacular instances where people have been kept alive for long periods of time on machines. The class said that this was an immoral act. It was a violation of this person's dignity, and it was morally wrong to keep them alive and not let them die. So in this instance they would say it's morally right to let this person die.

QUESTION: Do you really think that you can prepare yourself for death?

DR. LEE: Oh, definitely! Not in the sense that when it comes I am going to have a fanfare or something of that sort. But after being in the ethics class, I am certain that I can tell a world of difference in my own attitudes toward death. And I would think that if people deal with the question of death throughout their lives, confront it rather than ignoring it, they do become very well prepared for it.

QUESTION: What if you're not ready—you don't want to talk about the subject of death? Suppose somebody close to you dies and you don't want to talk about it. What do you do if somebody else is trying to force you to talk about it?

DR. LEE: Well, that's a sort of touchy situation which I think you would have to decide for yourself. I wouldn't be willing to say it's morally wrong for you not to talk about it. I think, though, it is important for you to have the opportunity to talk about it, if you want. I think if you're in a family and the family is discussing a death, you are to some degree responsible for, at least, listening to the people who want to talk to you about the fact that one of the members of your family has died. I think that's an important function.

QUESTION: My mother was ill for sometime, and I knew that the end was coming. But it seemed like I couldn't give her up. A friend was with me one evening, just shortly before my mother passed away. My friend asked me if I had arrived at the point where I would be willing to give up my mother? I said, "No, in my heart I haven't, because I don't see how I can." My friend said, "Well, that is one thing you must prepare yourself for." Later after prayer, I felt I got perfect release. Is it wrong to feel that way in your heart when you don't see how you can give people up?

DR. LEE: No, I think your experience was that you really did confront the death issue. You were willing to talk about it, and that is liberating in itself. We seem to dread death so much that we don't want to talk about it. But when you did confront it, you found that you were liberated. It's never easy though to confront the fact that your beloved mother is dying.

RESPONSE: Well, it just seemed like I couldn't accept it, but after I did, I seemed to have perfect relief and was happy. It so happened that she did pass away the next day.

QUESTION: I have not experienced in my lifetime the loss of a person that I was really close to, and I feel like I'm really insensitive to death. No one knows how he may really react. Is there a way that I can prepare myself for the death of a loved one?

DR. LEE: I don't know other than just an openness to confront the issue. It doesn't sound like you're hiding from the issue if you are willing to confront it whenever it comes. One of the problems the students had within their own families was with the people who wouldn't let them confront death, who wouldn't even talk to them, or who ignored or rejected them. It doesn't sound like you're doing that. It sounds like you're willing to confront the issue. I think that is all I'm saying at this point: You should confront death when it comes, and you should not be afraid of it. You should be totally open.

QUESTION: It's hard for me to realize what death is going to be like, and if you haven't experienced it, you don't know what to expect.

DR. LEE: The only people who do know are dead. If your attitude is one of looking forward to one of the basic experiences of life, then it may be that this kind of attitude, or the desire to develop that kind of openness to the experience, is about all you can hope for.

DR. LEE: Can I ask them a question?

DR. TUCK: Certainly.

DR. LEE: How do you react to the idea of letting people die if they choose to die? I never quite knew how to respond to the class on this subject, and I would be curious as to some of your reactions. I read a letter in class about a person who was perfectly healthy, but she wanted to die. She had completed everything that she wanted to do in life and was in good health, and yet she chose to die. The ethics class was sympathetic with the idea that this person should be allowed to die and not be condemned by society for this wish. The person who wrote the letter said that the only reason she didn't find some means of suicide was because it would be so totally unaccepted socially. She was a Christian, and she said, "I'm not doing it because of the flak that my family would get if I did do it." I would be curious to know your reaction to that. I was dumbfounded in some ways.

RESPONSE: Could not death be used here simply as an escape, just as we use other things for an escape? I think we have to look at perhaps some of the reasons people want to die. For instance, my grandmother lived a number of years as an invalid, and she had lived a full Christian life. She really had no desire to live because she felt that she could no longer be an active person. However, when she died we were unhappy for ourselves because we no longer had Grandmother; but we were happy for her because she was released from her suffering. But she did not want to use death as an escape, and I think death sometimes can be used as an escape.

DR. LEE: But, would it necessarily have been an escape if she said, "I would choose to die." Does it have to be an escape to do that?

RESPONSE: No, no, and in her case I do not think, if she had expressed a desire to die, that it would have been an escape. I do believe that this could be a moral issue because sometimes a person may choose to die rather than face life.

QUESTION: Was the letter you referred to written by an older person?

DR. LEE: Yes, I think the letter was written by a person who was in her nineties. But now, you see, if you allow one person freedom to choose the time of his own death, then you must allow others that same freedom.

QUESTION: If we permit people to have the freedom to experience death, where there is no medical or physical issue involved, wouldn't we be giving them the same kind of freedom which the anarchist says he should have in society? He claims he doesn't want to live under the laws of civilization. Wouldn't there be a parallel?

DR. LEE: The anarchist is usually doing damage to other people, even physical damage. This person is simply electing to eliminate himself from society.

QUESTION: Are you saying that freedom to die is similar to the anarchist?

DR. LEE: I'm not so sure. If the person has the agreement of his family—assume that a family would agree to let the person die—I don't see where it would be damaging to society in terms of physical damage like an anarchist. I'd like to pursue that more with you. Were you saying that you could not allow this person to choose death?

RESPONSE: It seems to me that if you're permitting a person to die, where no physical question would be involved in it, then they just stop living. If they use an artificial means to bring about death, then I think it would be morally wrong for them and for the family or for society. Because this would be breaking the laws of society, just as we might break the laws in other ways. But if the family chose not to use any artificial means to keep the person alive and allowed him to die of natural causes without sustaining him by some outside control, then I think the family has the right to make that kind of choice.

DR. LEE: I understand your point. Thank you.

7

A Physician Looks at Death

I will share briefly with you some of the things that physicians generally believe regarding life and death. Although I am giving my own opinion, I think that I speak for physicians in general in many of the things that I'll say. I'll try to keep the medical terms at a minimum, but in order to put my comments in perspective, I want to say a few things about how we live. Then I'll mention a few things about how death occurs and what we as physicians try to do to keep it from happening. I think that's what it's really all about.

When you stop and think about it, you realize that the human body is the most complex of God's creations. The simple matter of my moving my eyes from the front row to the back row of this church sanctuary involves the instant operation of some fourteen to sixteen muscles, numerous chemical reactions, and electrical impulses. The mere matter of hearing sounds involves the changing of sound energy from a gaseous to a fluid medium, from air to water, and then to electrical impulses. Almost everything we do involves complex chemical reactions.

From the time of birth until the time of death, there's a constant replenishing of the body's cellular structure. As old cells die, new ones are developed in their place. If you get a suntan and your skin sheds, new skin comes under it. That's all part of a big process. The important life processes have to do with breathing (this is one of the few things that although it is involuntary, you can control it somewhat) but if you go to sleep, you still breathe. Circulation is another important process—as the heart pumps, the blood circulates. Nutrition is the converting of food to energy, which is then circulated to all parts of your body. Finally the brain functions and makes a decision. All these things are both voluntary and involuntary, and they have to do with life processes.

Well, what causes death, then? Usually the first book that a medical student buys when he enters medical school is Dorland's *Medical Dictionary*. It defines death as "the apparent extinction of life as manifested by absence of heartbeat and respiration." Respiration, of course, is breathing. Anything that interferes with any of the life processes, anything that will destroy any one of them, anything that makes an individual stop breathing causes death if nothing is done to prevent it. Anything that causes the circulation to stop, whether it be a heart attack, an accidental electrocution, or some other will cause death. Injuries cause death in such a way as to interfere with these normal and essential life processes. Tumors cause death by their manner of growth; by the way they invade important body structures, stop these structures from functioning, and eventually overtake these important structures. In a nutshell, this is the background as to what causes death.

Now, what do physicians do to try to prevent this? In summary physicians aid and advise their patients in their fight against illness. There are all degrees of illness, but whether it be a minor or major degree of illness, your body still puts up some degree of fight or defense against this. All the physician can do is to help you in your defense, whether it be by simply giving advice to the overweight patient who must lose weight to control his diabetes or high blood pressure or by prescribing medication, such as digitalis to prevent heart failure.

By the judicious application of chemical principles, by using medication, certain of the important body functions which I have mentioned are altered or aided. The patient who is a diabetic, who doesn't have insulin, is given insulin in calculated dosages from outside the body. But the body still works, and this patient is able to carry on a normal life. There is, also, the surgical field whereby things which are abnormal in the body or which are causing illness are remedied or altered. The life-threatening tumor is removed, hopefully completely. The ruptured blood vessel which is causing the loss of circulation is repaired surgically. The bleeding ulcer is stopped.

With advice, medication, and surgery, we try to help the patient overcome his illness. I think this is what almost all physicians are dedicated to; the principle of aiding the patient in his fight against illness. When life-threatening illnesses are involved and the patient and the doctor lose the fight, then death occurs.

Dr. Tuck has said that no one could accept death graciously. I think physicians do not accept death graciously because we always hold out hope that tomorrow the cure for cancer will be developed or some new drug will come out and prolong life. This is how things have been so far. Another thing that was brought out earlier was the way that our general society will camouflage death. Physicians and hospitals, of course, do that, too. I'm not saying it is the best thing to do, but it's a fact of life. When a patient dies in the hospital, he is brought down the back elevator. The morgue, in every hospital where I have been, is in the basement. The autopsy room is in the basement, and when the hearse comes, it always comes to the back door. Camouflage is certainly a very real thing.

I think there is perhaps a great difference in the way the physician and lay people approach death and live with it. I suppose it's a matter of exposure. Physicians try to be objective with regard to their treatment, even in hopeless situations. But because of the fact that they live with death, day in and day out, they are able to approach the subject of death more objectively. I think the physician's relationship to death is to fight as hard as he can to prevent it. I think I'll conclude here, and I can't wait for the questions you've got to ask me.

DR. TUCK: I have a few questions which have come to my mind. Would you say that doctors generally see death as a sort of defeat in their attempt to work with a person?

DR. CROCKETT: Well, speaking for myself, yes. Of course, some patients that come are obviously hopelessly ill from the beginning, but we still try. I think not many doctors take it personally, but

I do think we all look on death as something we'd like not to happen.

DR. TUCK: Kubler-Ross has done a detailed study with dying people in a book entitled, *On Death and Dying,* and she says that "it's not: *Should we tell* people they are dying but *how* do we tell them." Do you agree with that?

DR. CROCKETT: Yes, my experience has been that it isn't very often that you have to tell people. The greatest majority of the patients know. I don't know how or why, but the greatest majority will have the sensation that things have not gone right and the end is somewhat inevitable. But I would agree in principle with this, yes.

DR. TUCK: What I have sensed in my own experience, and with some doctors and even with ministers, is that we sometimes play a little game with the dying patient. Everybody pretends that he's really not dying. He knows it. We know it, but we never talk about it. May this not be the last real denial we can give him of personhood? Do you agree that we really ought to try to talk about death with the patient?

DR. CROCKETT: Yes, I think so. I completely agree with that statement. I wonder, as do all physicians, who will decide in the last analysis, to pull the plug on the respirator? Do you understand? The definition of death I gave is a long standing one. As you know with so much controversy over the transplants, etc., some legal cases have arisen because the heart has been taken out of somebody who was believed not to be dead. One might speak of brain death, for example, where the brain wave on the electroencephalogram shows no electrical activity. A flat EEG, where there's no wave or a motion, in many places has been used as a legal definition for death. I've seen cases at many hospitals where a patient would have this, no electrical activity of the brain whatsoever, but yet was being maintained by a respirator and the heart would continue to beat. But who's going to pull the plug on the respirator? I'm not.

DR. TUCK: Do you not feel that there is a responsibility for somebody at this stage to talk with the family? If the doctor doesn't or will not, should not someone, whether he is the minister or somebody else, reveal to the family that all they have here is a "medical life"?

DR. CROCKETT: Well, I think in every case the physician talks this over with the family, and usually they are not kept on the artificial equipment very long. But I know of no case where that would not be communicated with the family.

DR. TUCK: Would you convey to me, if this were my family member, whether or not you think the plug should be pulled or would you let me make that decision?

DR. CROCKETT: I'd probably tend to say that it's a matter of individual preference, and perhaps in truth, I might not tell you everything in a situation like that. I don't think that in an absolutely hopeless situation, obviously hopeless where not even a breakthrough tomorrow would make any difference, that it would be right to prolong uselessly the hospitalization and the expense by simply giving intravenous feedings. I have seen, as all physicians have, what have been rather miraculous recoveries.

DR. TUCK: I think we've all seen instances in which everybody thinks a person is hopeless. They may have cancer, or something else, and no one thinks they will live very long. Then the first thing you know they are back working. They appear well and healthy. I'm certain you do not claim to be omnipotent in your judgments.

DR. CROCKETT: No, no. I think that's why we always hold out to the last possible hope.

DR. TUCK: What are your own feelings about euthanasia or mercy killing? Do you think there is a point where death should be administered? Some people say that we don't let our horses or animals suffer, why should we let a person suffer continually and indefinitely? Do you think there is a point, even if the patient has his rational faculties but he is suffering miserably without hope, where life should be terminated?

DR. CROCKETT: Well, I think that perhaps there is, but I would not be one who at this time would support it. There's really no reason for anybody to suffer with all the medication that we have today. I would be against taking another person's life. I would not be willing to assume that responsibility. I think that rests with the Higher Power.

DR. TUCK: What do you think the ordinary person can do to help someone, perhaps, in their family, who is dying? From your viewpoint, what can they do as concerned members of the family to assist their members in the process of dying?

DR. CROCKETT: That's a tough question. Number one, don't ignore the fact and hide your head. Number two, don't be particularly overindulgent. Don't try to make up for all the shortcomings that might have occurred in your relations with this individual. Act as naturally as possible, because that's really what I'd want if I were in that situation. I wouldn't want people hanging around me saying: "What can I do for you?" I think just act toward them as you would want them to act toward you if you were in their position.

QUESTION: Do people with devout Christian faith get well any more rapidly or require less medication to obtain a desirable result?

DR. CROCKETT: No, I don't think there's any difference. Sorry, but I don't think so. I think that they approach illness and death in a far better fashion, with perhaps a better attitude, but as far as healing per se goes, I don't think there's any difference.

QUESTION: Do you believe in faith healing?

DR. CROCKETT: Dr. Tuck and I were discussing a little earlier the unfathomed resources in the mind and some of the things that can occur under deep hypnosis. Yes, I believe that in certain ways some faith healing does take place. Now, without going off the deep end, I'd qualify that to say that I think there are some things that can be healed and some that can't. A great majority of the illnesses that we see today are psychosomatic, but I think that a certain amount of faith healing does occur.

QUESTION: How does a physician know when the outcome is hopeless?

DR. CROCKETT: Our earlier discussion concerned who is going to be the one to make the final decision. Every case has to be individualized. I, for one, and I think most physicians feel that prolonged maintenance of life with artificial means—respirator and this type of thing, when there's no hope, when there's no spontaneous life otherwise—is probably unwise over a long period of time. There is a certain period of time where you really don't know, but after awhile you do begin to know. And each one has to make up his own mind individually at that time.

QUESTION: Can the physician pull the respirator plug if he wants to?

DR. CROCKETT: Well, I think probably so. Yes, if he wants to take it upon himself.

QUESTION: Do many families want life prolonged needlessly?

DR. CROCKETT: I think that in the majority of cases of this type that usually the family will not want the life prolonged needlessly.

QUESTION: Have you ever heard the term "no heroics" used on a terminal patient's chart?

DR. CROCKETT: Many times. That's more or less an informal term that a great many people use. I guess an analogy would be somebody who may have a particular type of tumor that's beyond the extent of medicine or surgery or X-ray, and you know that sooner or later this is probably going to erode a large blood vessel and the patient will die from this. Well, when this happens do you get all the blood you can get and pump it back in the patient endlessly? That would be a heroic effort. In a situation like that one person might say to another, "No heroics." I've never heard it mentioned that a patient would say that. On the other hand, there is certainly a place for heroic and quick action, but that's not what we're talking about here.

QUESTION: Do you classify euthanasia and the cessation of prolongation of life by artificial means the same?

DR. CROCKETT: No, I think that I would classify them as two separate and distinct areas completely without any overlap. There's a difference in letting a person die or making him die. That's the difference we're talking about. In no conferences where I have ever been has there ever been any discussion or promotion of euthanasia. It's totally out of the question. I have never, in the medical meetings I have been in, really heard it discussed with any substance. I think it is mostly a philosophical discussion. It goes against everything that we're taught to do.

QUESTION: Do you know any physicians who are faith healers?

DR. CROCKETT: I know a great many physicians who are very devoted Christian physicians, but the combination of physician and faith-healer—I do not know any of them.

QUESTION: Do you think a person can heal himself by his own faith?

DR. CROCKETT: Well, of course, you know the Christian Science religion is based on this. Here again we must recognize what we said before: the untapped resources of the mind. I certainly would not say it could not occur. It just doesn't very often.

QUESTION: What would you say is the most traumatic reaction that most people usually have when they find out that they are dying or that someone else, such as their loved one, is dying?

DR. CROCKETT: The initial thing is, of course, shock. But in my experience most people accept it very well. It's a traumatic experience by definition, but as for one reaction being more traumatic than another, I couldn't tell you. To me, it has never been a real problem with people. Most all patients accept it, as do most families.

QUESTION: How do you predict how long someone will last with a terminal illness?

DR. CROCKETT: That's mostly done on television. You really don't know. I never even make a prediction. You can say if you know it's going to be days, weeks, or months; but when you get past that it's tough. It's just a guess.

QUESTION: We hear some people who are quite ill say, "I wish I could go on," or "I wish the Lord would take me." Is that a kind of death wish or is that a suicidal approach, or is it really a realistic approach if your life is really over?

DR. CROCKETT: I think that most people who make statements of that type, perhaps say it rather quickly and without much deep thought about what they're really saying.

QUESTION: Have you ever heard of a person coming back to

life?

DR. CROCKETT: There have been quite a few cases where the heart of a patient has stopped for a few moments and he has been revived by the doctor. But I know of only one case where someone has been dead for any long period of time and he has come back to life. It happened about two thousand years ago— Jesus Christ.

QUESTION: Are there instances of patients with terminal illnesses who do not want their life prolonged with artificial means?

DR. CROCKETT: Oh, I think so. I don't think we were talking awhile ago about this type of situation. I think that's a very valid wish. I think that there are people who just get tired of living, and I don't think there's any question about that. One thing I meant to say, and I didn't, was that one thing I think physicians try to do—and they are not always successful, because the situation isn't always ideal—but most physicians try to allow patients to die with dignity. I think that's the best way to put it. I think that's a meaningful desire for every patient.

8

A Funeral Director Looks at Death

As a funeral director, I want you to understand how I feel about death and how we think you see us in relation to death. I guess in self-defense, first of all, I want you to realize that we funeral directors are not in mourning. We can't be in mourning; we have to be alert and responsive to know what your needs are. If we were caught up emotionally in the funeral, then we wouldn't be able to help. We couldn't serve you as you deserve to be served. A person who has experienced a death in the family must be free of all outside problems so that he can start his grief work, so that he can adjust to this loss. It's our responsibility to see that these details are taken care of so that this can be done. This focuses on the importance of the funeral itself.

What does the funeral do and why is the funeral important? There are many reasons, but a few of the most important are:

1. It gives a person a chance to reminisce. They are brought face to face with the reality of death. Such reminiscence weakens the attachment, and this is what we must do. We must break this attachment and adjust to the loss. The funeral gives a chance for friends and relatives to gather and act as a cushion or a support for us while we are experiencing this detachment.

2. Crying is a very important part of detachment and an important part of the funeral. The funeral home says: "It's OK to cry here. This is the place where you can go ahead and cry." The funeral director must say verbally or nonverbally: "I'm comfortable with someone who's crying. I know what you're feeling. I know what your loss is; please don't be embarrassed." The funeral is really the ritual of termination. This is it; this is final; this is the end of being with the body.

American people all deny death, and this denial is seen on every hand. Jokes are made about death, and I wish sometimes that I could take the people who make death and funeral directors the butt of their jokes off into a corner and make them listen to these jokes over and over as many times as we do. Death is not funny, unless it doesn't happen, and with us it happens practically every day; therefore, we can't appreciate jokes about death.

3. The funeral director and the funeral itself are instrumental in the turning away from the dead to the living, of giving a person an opportunity to affirm the reality of the loss. The funeral director is responsible for the preventive medicine of mental illness. Not only mental illness, but doctors have even traced physical diseases to people who have not done their grief work. These are people who could not admit that they had lost someone or that death was real.

What I'm trying to say is that the funeral director as well as the funeral are very important when we find ourselves faced with the loss of someone who is close to us. The funeral gives us the opportunity to sever the ties with the physical body. I would hate to think that when any of my family dies that I would never have the opportunity to visit the grave, or to remember the times that we had had together. This is part of the function of a funeral, and this is why it is important to you and to me.

DR. TUCK: I remember when I was a boy a certain radio program used to refer to the funeral director as "Digger O'Dell," the friendly undertaker. What is your reaction to the kind of image which people so often have of the funeral director? People refer to you as an undertaker, or funeral director, or mortician; how would you like for people to see you?

MR. COOK: Well, I think that the accepted terminology would be "funeral director." Dad and I were discussing this term "undertaker" earlier today. Fifty years ago when someone died in the community with no funeral director there—the closest one being possibly miles and miles away—with no automobiles, no modern embalming equipment, it was an "undertaking," and somebody got stuck with it. That's exactly where that word came from, but our thinking is being manipulated today by television, movies, and books; therefore, I think the word "undertaker" fits, too. Everybody believes that an undertaker is very solemn, dresses in black, and has no sense of humor. It's just like the stereotype image people have about ministers who are supposed to eat more fried chicken than anyone else. Funeral directors are depicted in a stereotype mold; most of us, however, are not really like that.

DR. TUCK: Have you found that people do find death pretty distasteful? Are they difficult to deal with by the time they get to the funeral home because of this attitude?

MR. COOK: People are different. I'm sure you have discussed or will discuss with your congregation the different grief stages that people go through. For example, a family that has had someone ill for a very long time has had an opportunity to what you might call pre-grieve. They have already adjusted to their future loss. They know that it is coming and they are better situated to say: "Well, we know what's going to happen, and when it does happen we're not going to be upset about it. We hate for it to happen but it is inevitable." These people come in, and they are calm because they have done much of their grief work.

The people who are subjected to a severe loss or a very quick loss usually reflect many attitudes. Anger is one; they feel they have a right to be angry. They feel they have a right to demand that everyone be sorrowful. "My mother, or my wife, passed away yesterday, so why is that store still open? Why are they still operating? They are acting like nothing has happened. Why did the funeral director laugh when I walked into the funeral home to make funeral arrangements for my mother? There were several men standing in the foyer of the funeral home, and they were all laughing." Well, they weren't talking about this person's mother or anything connected with his family. They were merely passing the time of day when this person happened to pass by. But bereaved people don't see it this way.

The funeral director has to take all of these things into consideration and know that these people have a right to feel this way, and he needs to recognize that this is normal. This is a very normal reaction for a griever, and you have to be very careful in deciding what to do and how to handle it and then proceed as best you know how.

DR. TUCK: I think most of us are aware, as you indicated, that when somebody dies after a long illness, it does come as a kind of release to the family, since they have already, as you say, pre-grieved. How do you attempt to deal with these people who become almost uncontrollable because they have lost somebody quickly? How do you find that you are able to help them best?

MR. COOK: To say that every situation is different would be really an understatement because there are so many facets. A family, for instance, who has lost a child, especially if the child is older and the family is more aware that they will not be able to see the child grow older, mature, and get married, usually feels the greatest sense of loss. They feel cheated. "Why did God take *my* son, and this fellow I know who is a habitual drunk is the healthiest man on the block?" All of these questions go through their mind, and the best thing that you can do is to let them know that their feelings are normal, and that this, too, will pass.

DR. TUCK: Do you talk to them about their feelings of anger, guilt, and so forth or when they express the idea that their loss is "the will of God"?

MR. COOK: If they express it to us. The situation has come up on occasions when a family is in the chapel. The minister, of course, cannot be there all the time, and this would be a fine place for him to step in. But in a situation where a family is grieving and crying, and really broken up over this loss, and a well-meaning friend says: "Now, now, don't cry, don't cry," I can see myself very easily stepping in and saying: "It's perfectly all right for her to cry. She should be allowed to cry."

DR. TUCK: I really liked what you said about giving people the feeling that the funeral home is a place where they can weep. Weeping is a natural outlet, and I have found, and I'm sure all have found, many people who really become ill, emotionally, psychologically, and physically because they have no way to vent their emotions.

MR. COOK: There are different reasons for grief. Many times there is a certain amount of guilt, sometimes it is warranted, sometimes not. They feel like they didn't do what they should have done while "so-and-so" was alive, so this is a way of showing how sorrowful they are. We have to guard against this when a family selects a funeral and a casket. They come into the funeral home, and we show them our selection, but we have to watch that this person doesn't, because of his guilt feeling, get something that he can't afford. He shouldn't jeopardize his life later on or his children's lives by getting something beyond his means. It takes a little talking sometimes to get them to understand that they shouldn't purchase the most expensive casket just because they feel like they didn't do enough for the person when he was alive.

DR. TUCK: Do you try, if possible, to keep them from turning the funeral into a big show and investing all of their life's savings in a casket that goes into the ground?

MR. COOK: Right.

DR. TUCK: Is there anything that you would suggest that families might do ahead of time to prepare themselves for a funeral?

MR. COOK: The people in this country are going to be faced in the next five or ten years with a mass of publications from the National Foundation of Funeral Directors. Many funeral homes have pamphlets which the National Foundation of Funeral Directors is sending out, and they are going to share them with anyone interested in receiving one. There are many ways in which prearranging is becoming more prevalent every day; it was not until this year that I personally handled a prearrangement for a funeral. I'm sure Dad had, but it was not the normal way to do it. I believe it is going to become the normal way to do it in the future. People who make arrangements this way aren't under pressure. They are not under stress, and they can take a more logical view of what they should buy, what they need, and then they're satisfied knowing it's done. It's going to be quite different.

Dr. Tuck: There are some who say: "Why should we even have a service?" Do you think that the funeral service itself really gives the family an opportunity to relieve their grief?

Mr. Cook: Immediately I say, "Sure, we need to have a funeral service," and everybody will say: "Why shouldn't he say that; he's in the funeral business. If we don't have funerals, he doesn't have a business." We would still have a business; there would still be receptacles; there would still be graves; there would still be some matter of disposition of the body; there would still be embalming for sanitary purposes. So really if we stopped the funeral itself, it would save us money. We wouldn't have to have a chapel; we wouldn't have to have visitation. We could just have a big storage room in the back.

As far as the funeral home is concerned, the funeral is of value only to the people who are left. It is a spiritual strengthening. One psychologist, in counseling some of his patients, found that some people were mentally upset when they did not have a funeral service, and this made it more difficult for them to adjust to their loss. Studies have found it was even beneficial for the griever to visit a funeral home and look at a perfect stranger in a casket and say: "Death is real, you know, it really happens to people. People really die."

My two sons see people die on television every day, and they have a problem distinguishing who really died, what actually happened. It is helpful for a child to attend a funeral and see, for example, his grandmother who may have died. First of all he may say: "Well, this is Grandmother, and she's dead." Secondly, it just clicks the switch. It does not let his little mind imagine or fantasize with psychedelic colors ideas about her like he's accustomed to seeing done on television. It stops it right there. This is it. This is Grandmother. She's dead. This is truly the more realistic approach.

Dr. Tuck: Often people try to hide children from death, and then the child would wonder what really happened to Grandmother or Mother.

MR. COOK: Some would say, "She's gone on a long visit. You'll see her some day."

DR. TUCK: They try to make death unreal.

MR. COOK: Right. And adults are very guilty of this.

DR. TUCK: There are many who feel that the funeral home may put too much emphasis on the body. It's cosmetically treated; it's embalmed, preserved, and yet from the Christian viewpoint, the body is not supposed to be the major concern if one believes in a life after death. Would you say that this kind of criticism is justified? How do you react to this?

MR. COOK: The cosmetology, or the make-up used, in the preparation of a body, is not in itself a denial of death, but in most cases is a denial of the manner of death. A person might have been in a bad automobile accident, or in a fire, for example. A little boy was badly burned and lived for several days in the hospital, and his mother and dad stayed around the clock with him. Yet when he finally died and his body was taken to the funeral home, the funeral director restored the little boy to as near his natural appearance as possible. When the family saw him, they made the remark that they were so relieved that, even though it didn't completely blot out the memory that had been etched in their mind of the poor little thing laying there in the hospital bed, it still kind of smoothed things over a little bit. They got to see him for the last time, and he looked very nice. He looked like their little boy. He looked well and healthy, and as they would have liked to have had him. Another example is older people who have been sick for months and months and have just wasted away. The amount of cosmetology that can be done to restore these people to as normal an appearance as possible just helps to relieve the feelings of the family. It does nothing for the body, and it's not done for the person who has died but for the people who are left.

DR. TUCK: In the light of what you said earlier about facing death, do you think that making a dead person look his "normal" self enables a family to face his death better, or is it not a sort of denial?

MR. COOK: I don't think cosmetology or the preparation of the body itself is in any way a denial of death. Here is the person and he is dead, but it denies to the family the manner of his death. It eases their mind regarding the way in which this person may have died. It takes away the scars of disease, sickness, or of accidents.

DR. TUCK: In 1963 Jessica Mitford wrote *The American Way of Death,* which was probably the most scathing denunciation of the funeral industry ever written. What would be your reaction, in a capsule, to some of her criticisms of the funeral industry?

MR. COOK: Well, I would like to change one word in what you said. I would trade "scathing" for "saving," because I think Jessica Mitford has done more for the funeral industry than any other person in the United States. She grabbed the funeral director by the nape of the neck, and she shook him good and hard and said: "This is what I've heard and seen." And the funeral director said, "Well, all right, let's see if this is really happening." The curbstoners and the "fly-by-night" people took to the woods, and she really purged the ranks and helped the dedicated funeral directors shake off the bonds that were placed upon them by people who just were not honest. Some of the examples in her book are absurd. There's no doubt about that to me, but as absurd as they were, it still made people ask questions. When she first wrote the book, funeral service dropped almost 25 percent that month, and memorial societies sprang up all over the United States. The following month the funeral service was back up to normal and the memorial societies all over the United States were floundering. They didn't provide what the people wanted. Some few did, but mostly in places like California.

QUESTION: In the cemeteries you are required by law to leave a perpetual maintenance fee. What about prearranged funerals? Do undertakers have to have a bond or some means to show that they will be in business three to five years from now?

MR. COOK: They did better than that. The federal government won't let us touch the money. If you come to the funeral home and purchase a funeral, no matter what the price is—let's just make a round figure—say $1,000.00, and you say: "Mr. Cook, this is what I want as far as a casket and a suit; my cemetery property is taken care of—all of the arrangements are made and we agree on a price of $1,000.00." Then you may say, "I want to pay you for that now." Well, I'll take your money and I'll give you a receipt for your money, but I will deposit that money that day in a trust fund in your name with a prearrangement form stating that the only way I can touch this money is by presenting your death certificate. Not only that, but you may go to the bank at any time and draw your money out under the rules of the bank, and not even inform me of it. The customer is in no way jeopardized, and this is why it is done.

Again this is another law that was passed because Jessica Mitford helped us. There were dishonest funeral directors, and they caused this sort of thing to be set up. There are some monies in the bank I would like to be using right now. They would help out a lot; nevertheless I know I'm not going to come up ten years from now and get caught short and have you come back and ask me for something which I can't furnish.

QUESTION: You mentioned in passing about people who might have parts of the body which they wanted to donate at their death. What are the procedures for dealing with this?

MR. COOK: Yes, there are certain laws and forms that must be filled out. Let us take, for example, a donor organ such as a kidney. First of all, it's got to be usable. The funeral director risks the embarrassment of a husband or wife who may say, "Fred and I talked about this and we want to give 'so-and-so' to science or to be a donor for a transplant." The funeral director may have to say, "Well, that's fine, but let's discuss it." Whatever forms are necessary are signed but even then the hospital or college may still turn the donor down. Here's where you've got to go back to the husband or wife, who felt so very good about this, and who may have already spent money with you, and say, "They don't want Fred. He's too fat." We will investigate the donor procedures with them, and if this is what they still want, they should also keep in mind that there are so many thousands of people doing this that they have to be a pretty good specimen.

QUESTION: If a person wants to donate an organ, say his eyes, will they have to be used almost immediately or removed immediately?

MR. COOK: If it were done, it would have to be done on a prearrangement, as you can see. Let's take a hypothetical case: Someone may be in the hospital from a bad automobile accident, and they had stated previously that if anything like this should happen to them, they would like to donate their heart, kidney, or some other organ, if it were possible. The family thinks this is what he really wanted to do, although he's still alive at the moment, and his body organs are still healthy and functioning. But the doctor says there is no chance for his survival. He will die; it's just a matter of two or three days. The proper forms should then be filled out so the hospital will be ready to receive this donor's organ. At the time of death, the organ is taken from the body, and then the funeral director is called, and the body is picked up and embalmed. The funeral is held and everything is just as normal.

The same thing is even true for the total body. A man and wife may have decided that they would like to give their bodies to an anatomical college upon death, and they have filled out the necessary papers and everything beforehand. The husband dies first. The wife, then, calls the proper authorities, maybe without even consulting a funeral director. She could have called on the funeral director for transportation, but, let's just say, that she called the college directly, and the college made what we refer to as the first call and picked up the body and carried it themselves to the college.

Once, for example, thirty days after a woman had done this she called the college and said: "I want my husband back." And she retrieved the body and had a funeral and put him in a cemetery; and she said that for thirty days she had thought about never being able to visit the grave and the different aspects that were connected with just having the body gone. However, if a person is psychologically ready to accept this type of thing, and they would still like to have the funeral, this is fine. The body can be prepared, embalmed, the funeral held, and then as far as disposition of the body is concerned, it would be sent to the college or the place of the family's choice.

QUESTION: I have a question concerning the prearranged funeral. The cost that you used, the round figure of $1,000.00, at today's prices is this to buy a certain quality of casket or a certain quality of funeral? Fifteen years from now, $1,000.00 at the rate it's going, is not going to buy very much. Are you still going to furnish the same quality funeral?

MR. COOK: We are required to state on the form what quality the casket will be, and we are hoping that by placing this money in trust, under a ninety-day withdrawal, at 5 percent interest, this will cover the inflationary trend. Now, just as everything else, this is more or less a gamble. The form also says that, "This money is to be applied to the funeral expenses of Mr. Blank." At the end of ten years, this person might come back and say: "My husband just passed away and we had prearrangement." We get the prearrangement form out, and it is fully stated (it's not a loophole but merely a mutual agreement) that if the inflationary process has gone out of sight and there's no way we can reach it with the money that was put away for this, then we must renegotiate with the person who has made the prearrangement.

But they still have the choice of saying, "Well, we don't want this. We'll go some place else." Even though we've made the call, have the body in the funeral home, and are sitting in the arrangement room making the arrangements, if they want to change their mind, they are perfectly free to do so. It is not binding on them. It's by no means binding as far as the person needing the prearrangement, or making the prearrangement. But it does protect the funeral director in the sense that we couldn't sell a funeral today for $500, have the person live for twenty-five years, and expect to get the same kind of funeral if the present inflationary trend continues.

QUESTION: What happens if someone dies, and they have no relatives or do not have the money to be buried?

MR. COOK: In most states, welfare pays a small amount of the expenses. But in most instances, the funeral home bears the cost. It's like any other business; you've got to take the good with the bad, and you can't turn people down and feel morally right. People have always had the idea that when a person walks into the funeral home that the funeral director has you at his mercy. Suppose someone in your family has died, and you come to the funeral director feeling that he is going to take everything you've got, and everything that's left. But what in reality has happened is that, when you walk into the door, you have the advantage because he must do what you say. He knows your situation and he can't say: "Well, you come back next week. I've got to run a credit check on you." He can't say, "If that's all the money you've got in your pocket, you'll have to go some place else." He must sit down and make arrangements with you, letting you tell him your circumstances and decide whether or not you're doing the right thing, if you're really doing what you want to, and whether you can afford to do it. It's not just a question of trying to sell somebody a $3,500, $4,500, or $5,500 funeral.

MR. COOK (*to the congregation*):   I have two questions for you: Did any of you feel badly about coming to church tonight or last Sunday night because of this particular series? Now really, be honest with me. Did it scare any of you? Did you worry about something that might be said that would upset you? What would you think about a study being initiated in a high school on the senior level on various perspectives of death? This way you would be able to find out what goes on in a funeral service, the different things which should be done prior to a funeral, during a funeral, and after the funeral. All of you that think it would be all right—let me see a show of hands, and be honest.
RESPONSE: (*A very positive yes.*)
DR. TUCK: One of the most disturbing things ministers feel about the funeral concerns the setting of the time by funeral directors without consulting the ministers beforehand. The minister may be out of town or have other things scheduled, and the time is

set, sometimes it is even published in the paper, and then the minister is informed when the funeral service is to be. As you can imagine some of them get rather upset. They feel it deters them from ministering properly to the family. Is there some way we can overcome this problem?

MR. COOK: Ninety percent of the time when I'm taking the information to fill out a death certificate, what we call the work sheet, I turn the work sheet over and write the name of the deceased, and the second item is: Date and time of service. Then I ask: "Have you all talked with your pastor about when you want the service?" If they say, "Yes, we have, and he can do it Tuesday afternoon at two o'clock or Monday morning at eleven," we set it at that time if there is no conflict with our schedule. If they say, "No, we called him and he was out," then I say: "Well, let me call now. What hour would you like it?" They may say, "We'd like to have it Tuesday at two." Then I call and check with the minister. If he is not there and his secretary can't confirm this, then I ask him to call me and we set a tentative time, and leave the arrangements incomplete.

This is the only way it can work. We feel the burden should be on us; we are the ones who have the people in the arrangement room, and we talk to them nine times out of ten before anybody else does. We have to have the trust of the minister, and we want to try to check with him before any final plans are made.

QUESTION: Is there a general trend in the future because of the scarcity of land to turn toward cremation?

MR. COOK: It has been said that if everyone who has died since the birth of Christ was placed in Texas, they would have approximately three square yards of empty ground left. The population is increasing, and it's increasing faster than we think. As far as cremation is concerned, I think this may have religious connection for some, but as far as the funeral directors are concerned, cremation is neither pro nor con with us. We will still have work to do. Someone must transport the body; the body still has to be embalmed, unless it's going to be cremated within a certain time. It has to reach its destination within thirty hours. We still feel like people are going to want the funeral with the body present, even though cremation takes place, or even if they use a mausoleum or crypt.

As far as trying to sway the public, we are trying to help the public to see the importance of the funeral with the body present. We believe this is psychologically healthy. This is what they need for healthy lives after they have lost someone. Again this isn't just promoting the business as such because the funeral business is going to be here. We need certain traditions and customs and if we didn't have them, we would need to invent new rituals and protect them, such as the funeral, or marriage, or home life, or the church. These are going to have to be roped off, and we are going to have to say: "Now, wait a minute, change is good, but there are certain areas which we do want to remain the same. I think we will keep the funeral. We need it."

9

A Lawyer Looks at Death

Death and the law is a most important concern for all of us as individuals and especially, I feel, as Christians. I understand you have heard in previous sessions various aspects of death and the problems that are caused by such. I hope our particular subject will fit right in with what you have covered. Speaking of the law and living and dying with regard to property and possession of property reminds me of a verse of Scripture. In 1 Peter 4:10 we find that we are to be: "good stewards of the manifold grace of God" (KJV). That would be interpreted by me, this way: that we—you and I—are entrusted by God with many material blessings. We are not worthy of these blessings necessarily, but they were not given to us by God because of our worthiness but because of our needs. If this is the case, and I think it is, God does give us, through his grace, many material blessings. He entrusts us with them because we need them, not because we are worthy of them. With this in mind let's consider how you and I, as Christian stewards, should take care of our possessions which have been given to us during the period of time that we are privileged to live on this earth.

Most adults spend about one-third of their life working to make a living: to make some money and maybe to take care of their family, their needs, and to buy certain things they would like to have; to accumulate a little money or a little property to be used during their lifetime. Most of us, as we grow into adulthood, try to use some of our money for the training and the education and the preparation of our children for a better life, we hope, than we had or, at least, as good a life as we feel that we have had. Many times we try to save money or obtain property or

135

things and to take time to accumulate money for the purpose of enjoying it for ourselves as hobbies. Sometimes our efforts may be for the benefit of others around us. But we are all interested in things to some extent for many of the reasons mentioned. And yet while we spend time and money during our life to obtain property, to use it, to enjoy it, we should also give consideration to that time when our earthly life ends. Many of us do not take time to think about what we're going to do about the property we possess or what is going to happen to it when we're no longer around to enjoy it or to use it.

Let's think about this subject of death and the laws affecting our property. Many times persons stop by a lawyer's office—sometimes couples, sometimes individuals, sometimes young, sometimes old—and they want to know the answers to questions concerning the transfer and disposition of property at the time of their death. They will say words to this effect: "We don't have much money and very little property so we wonder if there is any real use of having a will? Why not let our property pass, by law, whatever that might be, rather than make a will? Can you give us any good reasons why we should have a will? We have a house and lot, and it is in both of our names. We have a bank account in both our names, or maybe in one or the other of our names, and that's about all. What difference does it make whether or not we have a will?"

As you would expect, there are many things to consider in attempting to answer questions such as these. We are all aware that the various states of the Union have their own laws involving questions concerning wills and inheritance so what may be true in one state may not apply in another state. Being citizens of Bristol, as most of us here are, we have the unique situation, especially in the law profession, of being concerned with the laws of *two* states, Virginia and Tennessee. Let us approach these questions on a general basis and see if we can come up with some answers that would be helpful.

Why is it advantageous in many cases to have a will rather than to allow property and other matters involving death to be decided by the laws of a particular state? First, a will gives you the opportunity to decide how your property—whether of large or small value, whether personal property or real estate—shall pass at the time of your death. If you do not make a will, as I mentioned previously, your property will pass according to the laws of the state where you reside at the time of your death. Under certain situations, the results may be no different whether or not you have a will. Under most circumstances, however, there will be a difference in these results if you do or do not have a will at the time of your death.

In some states, for example, where there is a survivorship-type law in which the property owned by a husband and wife is involved, the surviving husband or wife shall receive any real estate owned jointly by them. In other states, however, where there is survivorship-type law, the property passes instead of to the surviving husband or wife, to the surviving children of the parties. You can realize how some problems might arise where a husband would like for his house and lot, for example, to pass to his wife, but having no will, his interest in the house and lot would pass by law to his children. You might have a situation where these children would be under the age of eighteen, and therefore not adults, and this would create problems concerning the disposing of property of minors by deed or will. By having a will, this situation would not arise, and, therefore, problems involving interest of minor children would not arise. In some states where the survivorship law is not in force, in the event the couple left no surviving children, the property might pass to the decedent's brothers and sisters, parents, nephews, or nieces before it would finally become the property of the surviving husband or wife.

As you can see, in certain cases where there is no will, a widow could conceivably be left out of any inheritance of real estate from the property of her deceased husband, as well as a good portion of the personal property. This would include money, stocks, or bonds which she might need in order to have a decent income and standard of living following the death of her husband.

You can see very quickly the importance of having a valid will at the time of your death.

A second advantage of having a will is that many times it provides for a saving of money in the form of taxes and other expenses. I know you are aware that both the Federal and the state governments have certain inheritance or estate taxes which are to be paid at the time of a person's death. From the Federal Government's standpoint, a person with a valid will with a fairly large estate, in excess of let's say $150,000, may be able to save a considerable amount of Federal estate taxes by taking advantage of what is called a marital deduction. This deduction is allowed where a husband or wife leave at least one-half of their estate to the survivor of the two of them. Without a will this marital deduction is not available and, especially in large estates, can amount to several thousand dollars in savings where the amount of the deduction is used.

Under certain circumstances in some states, there is also the possibility that property might pass from the decedent to a Class B beneficiary rather than to a Class A beneficiary which means a tax at a higher rate. (A Class A beneficiary would be a surviving husband or wife and children. A Class B beneficiary would be any other person receiving inheritance other than children and husband and wife.) For example, under certain cases property might pass by law to a widow, or it might pass to a brother or sister or some person considered under the law to be a Class B beneficiary. Instead of paying an inheritance tax of approximately $1\frac{1}{2}$ percent up to $50,000 in the estate value, it might be around 5 percent in that classification.

Class A beneficiaries usually receive a higher amount of exemption under state laws. For example, in some states a Class A beneficiary might have received an exemption of up to $10,000, while a Class B beneficiary might receive around $1,000. As you can see, the exemptions can mean a great deal with regard to the amount of taxes that might be due to the various states as well as to the Federal Government. Therefore, by having a will you may be able to save a considerable amount of money from the standpoint of taxes.

A will in many cases will also provide ways of cutting down or eliminating administrative expenses. As you may know, after a person dies someone has to be appointed executor or administrator of the estate of the deceased person. Many times states require that bonds be executed by the person qualifying as an administrator or executor, and this bond must be guaranteed or secured by a bonding company. Naturally, bonding companies require a fee or premium for this additional security. By having a will, this bonding security can be waived. I have seen many cases where the premium on the bond might amount up to $400 or $500. This could have been saved with no danger to the estate by having a waiver in the will, providing that no surety on the bond would be required.

Another advantage in having a will is that the decedent can provide in his will for the appointment of a person or persons or institution whom he feels is best qualified and whom he would prefer to administer his estate. Furthermore, a will can also designate certain powers that the executor, administrator, guardian, or trustee might have which would help in settling the estate in the most efficient manner. Without a will there are no powers given to the administrator of an estate, for example, which would allow him to sell real estate owned by the parties. This power of sale in the hands of an executor or trustee would be very important where you are dealing with beneficiaries who might be minors or persons who are unable to handle their own affairs due to their age or mental incompetence.

I think it is also important to consider the appointment of a guardian for minor children, which can be taken care of in the provisions of a will. Here again, a guardian can be given certain powers to manage correctly the property left to minor heirs during the time they are under the age of eighteen. This would include such powers as the right of a guardian to spend income from the inheritance for their adequate support, maintenance, and education. If this particular power is not given to the guardian through the will, it sometimes becomes a costly item to have to obtain a court approval by a guardian in order to spend money for the education and support of a minor.

In summary, some of the advantages of your having a will are: (1) to dispose of your property the way you want it to be disposed of; (2) possibly to save on inheritance taxes; (3) to save on administrative expenses; (4) to allow you to appoint the executor of your choice with certain powers to help handle the settlement of your estate in an efficient and as inexpensive manner as possible; (5) to allow you to name a guardian, if necessary for minor children, with powers necessary to protect and conserve the property that might be passing to these minor children.

As Christians, there is one further advantage, in my opinion, in having a will. You may want to leave your church or some charitable organization a gift at the time of your death. Without a will this cannot be done unless the gift is made prior to your death. The courts cannot set aside a certain amount of your money or property for a charity or religious institution unless you have provided for this in your will. I am sure many people, when they die would like to leave something to their church or to other worthy organizations for the benefit of the less fortunate. Without a will, however, this cannot be done. This opportunity for Christians to share some part of what they have received from God during their lifetime with people or institutions that can carry on programs or services that will have permanent meaning and benefits to mankind can only be accomplished through the use of a will. Laws of the state cannot make this possible.

DR. TUCK: I would like to ask a couple of questions and then we'll let our congregation ask some. You anticipated me on some of the questions that I had, which is good. Correct me if I'm wrong, but I sense from what you were saying that if a person doesn't have a will, it makes it much more complicated for his family after his death. Is that correct?

MR. COOPER: It can be. As previously mentioned, the fact that a person has expressed his wishes in writing concerning the disposition of his property and the designation of a person or persons to handle the administration of his estate can certainly reduce complications. Further, as I have stated, the powers granted to the administrator or executor also can reduce complications and also in many cases save expenses.

DR. TUCK: Could you distinguish for us the difference between the executor of the estate and the power of attorney?

MR. COOPER: Yes. A power of attorney is a legal instrument used to take care of a situation where a person might become temporarily disabled and needs someone to act for him. A power of attorney can be given to someone by this individual which permits that person to act for him in certain designated areas.

Sometimes it is necessary to appoint someone to act for another due to a person's mental capacity or qualifications. In this case there is a need for an appointment of a committee, which requires court approval. Many times due to age a person cannot take care of his affairs, and a committee is appointed in order to provide for the needs of that person from the standpoint of handling his financial affairs and looking after property. This is done as long as is necessary and up until the time a person should pass away.

The executor is named under the terms of a will, or an administrator is appointed where there is no will, after a person dies. This executor or administrator has the responsibility of settling up the estate of the person who died. The executor or administrator only serves during the period of administration after the death of someone. His term may last for a period of six to twelve months or longer depending on the length of time that is required to settle up an estate.

DR. TUCK: At my father-in-law's death my wife was to be the executor of the estate. Her family home is in Virginia but we live in Tennessee, and according to the law, as I understand it, she legally could not be the executor by herself. We had to have an attorney appointed. Are the variations in the law, from state to state, so complicated that without a will you can get into difficulty along this line?

MR. COOPER: Most states require that the executor or administrator named under the terms of the will must be a resident of that particular state where the will is probated. In other words, a person who dies leaving a will must have an executor or administrator who is a resident of the state where the person died and where his will was probated. It is possible that a person named in the will as executor, who might be a nonresident, may serve jointly with some person who is actually a resident of the state where the will is probated. Also, a problem sometimes arises where a person owns property in several different states. In this situation it may be necessary that a person be named as administrator in these various states in order to take care of the transfer of property after his death. So you can see that there are some complications involved in the settlement of the estate. And some of these complications can be eliminated or at least reduced by the naming of an executor.

DR. TUCK: I think this is another reason why we have found personally that an attorney can be very helpful in explaining these complications. And as mobile as our society is today, people need to be aware of the complications.

MR. COOPER: That's true.

DR. TUCK: Cannot a problem arise sometimes from a person putting money in certain types of securities, like government bonds, and, then, after his death the survivors discover that they cannot touch the securities? Would it not be better to check with an attorney to get some guidelines on what kind of securities one should invest his money in? Then his family could utilize it in the case of his death and would not be placed in such a perplexing position later.

MR. COOPER: That's right. It is important that persons realize that certain securities, such as bonds and notes and stock, may provide who the beneficiaries might be in the event of the death of the owner of these securities. If a bond, for example, provides a certain person as beneficiary, and at the same time the person's will leaves his property to other parties, you can see that there might be a conflict as to who would be entitled to receive the particular securities. A will cannot take priority over a security or legal instrument which provides on its face how such security should pass at the time of the death of the owner of that security. Therefore, if a bond, for example, is left by Mr. Jones to his brother and his will leaves all of his property including this bond to his wife, the designation set forth on the bond will control. It is very important that persons holding securities be certain to name beneficiaries on their securities that will not be in conflict with or inconsistent with the provisions of their will.

QUESTION: I would like to know the difference between a committee and a conservator.

MR. COOPER: I believe that both the conservator and the committee serve the same purpose: to take care of a person who by reason of advanced age or physical incapacity is incapable of managing his own estate. Both committee and conservator are appointed by the court. These are not handled by an ordinary legal document. It does require that a judge in a properly called proceeding actually make the appointment of a conservator or committee. The conservator or committee would be responsible for managing the estate of the person who was unable to handle the matter themselves. A bond would be required of the conservator or committee in order to be sure that the property of the person incapacitated would be protected.

QUESTION: Suppose someone made a will for their property and designated it to a certain person or a certain organization and the inheritance of this money was contingent upon the behavior of the person or whether or not a racial or ethnic group used this property—is this legally binding?

MR. COOPER: If the restriction should involve a constitutional issue then it would not be binding, in the event that the restriction was contested in court. In other words, if there was a restriction in a will concerning the receipt of money or property and the parties raised no question about this restriction, then there would be no problem. If, on the other hand, the restriction was contested by some party who might be interested in the property, then if it can be proven to be a constitutional violation it would be declared void. Such restrictions that might involve race, color, creed, or religion might possibly be found void if contested in a court.

QUESTION: Well, suppose they say if the person doesn't marry a Roman Catholic, or doesn't marry a Baptist, or something like that.

MR. COOPER: It is possible that a restriction concerning a matter of religion might be upheld. Again, it would depend upon whether or not there would be a violation of a person's constitutional rights to be deprived of property under the terms of a will due to a certain type restriction dealing with race, creed, color, or religion.

QUESTION: Suppose a person made his will to a charitable organization, such as the church or Boy Scouts, or some other organization. What are legal entanglements involving that? Would there be any taxes?

MR. COOPER: If you would report on your inheritance tax return that a will provided for the making of a gift to, let's say the Boy Scouts or YMCA, then it would be considered a charitable gift as far as the Internal Revenue Service is concerned. There are certain organizations that you might choose to give to which might not be considered charitable organizations. The question of charity is becoming more and more a point of contention. It may become necessary for persons who want to leave property to a charity to check with the Internal Revenue to be sure that the charities would meet with the necessary qualifications.

QUESTION: Suppose I would want to write my own will. Can I have somebody else write it, just so I sign it and have two witnesses for it?

MR. COOPER: Yes, you can have someone write your will for you or you can actually write the will yourself. If you should write your own will and sign it, there is no requirement under the law, at least as far as I know, that you have witnesses to acknowledge it. If you have someone else write your will out for you and you sign it, then you must have at least two witnesses to acknowledge your signature, both of the witnesses being present at the time you signed your name and present at the time that each witness signs his or her name. States differ as to the number of witnesses that must sign a will, and other matters concerning the proper way of signing and acknowledging a will.

QUESTION: What is the maximum amount you can get exempt from Federal estate taxes?

MR. COOPER: Every citizen of the United States is entitled to a $60,000 exemption from Federal and state taxes.

QUESTION: What would be the advantages of leaving part of your estate to charity, and under what conditions?

MR. COOPER: First of all, it may fulfill your desire and intent to leave money or other property to a worthy charity or religious institution whom you may designate in your will. Second, you receive benefits under state and Federal inheritance tax laws in the form of deductions from your inheritance taxes, which will, therefore, reduce your estate taxes.

QUESTION: Should a will always be probated?

MR. COOPER: The state laws require that the will of anyone dying must be offered for probate. It is not a question of whether you feel that it would be the best thing to do. The law requires that you must offer the will for probate.

QUESTION: If a will has been written out and the father dies and leaves a piece of property to his children—suppose he has, for example, eight children—how does he decide which particular one it would go to?

MR. COOPER: The person making the will, known as the testator, must decide how he wants his property divided among his survivors. He is not bound to leave it to any one person or in any proportionate amount to all of the survivors. It is up to the testator to decide what is best in the division of his property among his surviving family, friends, charities, and so forth.

QUESTION: Can life insurance be taxed? If so, what is the percentage of this tax, and does the state get some of this tax as well as the Federal Government?

MR. COOPER: Life insurance in which the testator retains some control over the policies is considered to be a part of his estate and is taxable as such just as other property is taxed. The percentage of taxation by the Federal and state governments is the same for insurance as any other property.

QUESTION: Are there any legal problems involved in inheritance tax in having a residence in one state and working in another?

MR. COOPER: Where you are employed has very little to do with inheritance taxes. In some cases, the state where you may have money deposited or property located might claim a tax on the property. State laws sometimes require that property can be removed from one state to another after a person's death through court approval in the state where the property is located.

QUESTION: Can your beneficiary be named executor?

MR. COOPER: Yes, there is no legal reason why this cannot be done.

QUESTION: Why would it not be, if your will is written in the usual manner, wife, children, etc., just as feasible to name your wife as executor as appointing an attorney or someone else?

MR. COOPER: This can be done and is done in many cases. Sometimes the settlement of an estate can become complicated, and it would probably be advantageous to name some individual or institution that is more qualified to handle this type of problem.

QUESTION: If the witnesses that you have on your will precede you in death, is your will still valid? Does that have any bearing?

MR. COOPER: If the witnesses to a will should die before the testator, the will can still be probated. The law may require that the handwriting of the testator be verified by other means. The will still remains valid, however.

QUESTION: Can you take the same will and get two new witnesses?

MR. COOPER: Yes, additional witnesses can be used if the testator properly acknowledges his signature before them.

QUESTION: This doesn't take the attorney's presence?

MR. COOPER: No, not necessarily.

QUESTION: Without getting into details or specific examples, what type of estate planning do you recommend to assist parents, in case of their death, that will take care of their young children?

MR. COOPER: Well, if a young couple has minor children, the

parents would want to provide for the appointment of a guardian for the children until they are at least eighteen years of age, at which time they are recognized as adults under the laws of most states. The will of the young couple can also provide that their guardian shall have certain powers which will allow for proper care for the children with a minimum of expenses, at least from the standpoint of court costs that might otherwise be required where there is no will.

QUESTION: Suppose there is no will and the only thing that a couple had done was to have joint ownership. What happens to the real and personal property?

MR. COOPER: Where there is no will, the disposition of property of a deceased person is controlled by the inheritance tax laws of the state in which the deceased is a resident at the time of his death. I would say in most states that joint ownership of bank accounts, stocks, bonds, and other securities would pass to the survivor in case of the death of one of the joint owners. Joint ownership of real estate would most likely go to the survivor or to the children, if any, of the deceased, depending upon the law of the state where the real estate is located. In the case of minors who might be the beneficiaries of bank accounts, bonds, etc., a guardian would have to be appointed by the court to manage this personal property until said minors reach their majority. In the case of real estate, the title to it passes immediately to the minors and the guardian would have no control over the real estate.

NOTES

PREFACE

1. Dow Kirkpatrick, ed., *The Finality of Christ* (Nashville: Abingdon Press, 1966), p. 172.

CHAPTER ONE

1. Morris West, *The Devil's Advocate* (New York: Dell Publishing Co., Inc., 1959), p. 5.

2. J. S. Whale, *Christian Doctrine* (London: Cambridge University Press, 1941), p. 171.

3. See "The Pornography of Death" by Geoffrey Gorer, *Death, Grief, and Mourning* (Garden City, New York: Doubleday and Co., 1967).

4. Karl Barth, *Church Dogmatics*, trans. A. T. Mackay, et. al., III, Part IV (Edinburgh: T. & T. Clark, 1961), p. 588.

5. Elizabeth Kübler-Ross, *On Death and Dying* (New York: The Macmillan Co., 1970), p. 28.

6. Halford E. Luccock, *Living Without Gloves* (New York: Oxford University Press, 1957), pp. 160-162.

7. H. C. Brown, Jr., *Walking Toward Your Fear* (Nashville: Broadman Press, 1972).

8. Carlyle Marney, *Faith in Conflict* (New York: Abingdon Press, 1957), p. 151.

9. John Donne, "Death Be Not Proud," in *Sunrise to Starlight*, compiled by May Detherage (New York: Abingdon Press, 1966), p. 195.

CHAPTER TWO

1. C. S. Lewis, *A Grief Observed* (New York: The Seabury Press, 1961), p. 7.

2. Cf. Erich Lindemann, "Symptomatology and Management of Acute Grief," *American Journal of Psychiatry*, 101 (September, 1944), pp. 141-148. Reprinted in *Journal of Pastoral Care*, 5 (Fall 1951), pp. 19-31.

3. *Ibid.*

4. Bernadine Kreis & Alice Pattie, *Up From Grief* (New York: The Seabury Press, 1969), pp. 13-15.

5. *Ibid.*, pp. 15-16.

6. Joshua Loth Liebman, *Peace of Mind* (New York: Simon and Schuster, Inc., 1946), p. 114.

7. Soren Kierkegaard, *The Concept of Dread*, trans. Walter Lowrie (Princeton

University Press, 1944), p. 96.

8. Kreis and Pattie, *op. cit.*, p. 17.

9. Cited in C. Charles Bachmann, *Ministering to the Grief Sufferer* (Englewood Cliffs, New Jersey: Prentice-Hall, 1964), p. 19.

10. Paul Tournier, *The Healing of Persons*, trans. Edwin Hudson (New York: Harper & Row, 1965), pp. 95-109.

11. Burton H. Throckmorton, Jr., "Do Christians Believe in Death?" *The Christian Century* (May 21, 1969, vol. LXXXVI, No. 21), p. 710.

12. Lewis, *op. cit.*, p. 16.

13. Edna St. Vincent Millay, *Collected Poems*, edited by Norma Millay (New York: Harper & Row), p. 241.

14. Kreis and Pattie, *op. cit.*, p. 51.

15. Edgar N. Jackson, *Understanding Grief* (New York: Abingdon Press, 1957), p. 154.

16. Kreis and Pattie, *op. cit.*, pp. 54-55.

17. Jackson, *op. cit.*, p. 175.

CHAPTER THREE

1. Robert Enrico, *An Occurrence at Owl Creek Bridge*, Filmartic and Films du Centaure for Cappagariff; McGraw-Hill, 1962. Based on a short story by Bierce Ambrose in *In the Midst of Life and Other Stories* (New York: Signet Books, 1961).

2. William Shakespeare, *As You Like It* (Act III—Sc. 5).

3. Charles Schulz, *Peanuts* (United Feature Syndicate, Inc., 1973).

4. Leslie Weatherhead, *Why Do Men Suffer?* (Nashville: Abingdon Press, 1936).

5. Paul Tournier, *To Understand Each Other* (Richmond: John Knox Press, 1968), p. 28.

6. Ashley Montagu, *Touching: The Human Significance of the Skin* (New York: Harper & Row, 1971), p. 1.

7. Dietrich Bonhoeffer, *Life Together* (New York: Harper & Row, 1954), p. 98.

8. John Sutherland Bonnell, *No Escape From Life* (New York: Harper & Row, 1958), pp. 61-64.

9. Bonhoeffer, *op. cit.*, p. 99.

10. *Ibid.*, p. 100.

11. Ted Husing, "I Could Not Hide from My Friends," *Guideposts* (New York: Guideposts Associates, Inc., April, 1960).

12. Sam Keen, *To a Dancing God* (New York: Harper & Row, 1970), p. 31.

13. C. S. Lewis, *A Grief Observed* (New York: The Seabury Press, 1961), p. 21.

14. John R. Claypool, "Does God Really Help in Trouble?" (Unpublished sermon delivered in Broadway Baptist Church, Fort Worth, Texas, October 8, 1972).

CHAPTER FOUR

1. Charles Schulz, *Peanuts* (United Feature Syndicate, Inc., 5-1-1973).

2. Ellen Glasgow, *The Wheel of Life* (New York: Doubleday, Page & Company, 1906), p. 454.

3. Albert Schweitzer, *Out of My Life and Thought*, trans. C. T. Campion

(New York: Henry Holt and Co., Inc., 1933), p. 103.

4. Helen Keller, *Three Days to See* (Pawling, New York: Foundation for Christian Living, n.d.), p. 11.

5. Fyodor Dostoyevsky, *The Idiot*, trans. Constance Garnett (New York: Random House, 1962), p. 55.

6. Thornton Wilder, *Our Town* (New York: Coward McCann, Inc., 1938), pp. 124-125.

7. Paul Tournier, *Learn to Grow Old* (New York: Harper & Row, 1972), p. 228.

8. Thomas Merton, *Contemplative Prayer* (New York: Herder and Herder, 1969), pp. 112-113.

9. *Ibid.*, p. 140.

10. Boris Pasternak, *Dr. Zhivago*, trans. Max Hayward and Manya Harari (New York: Pantheon Books, Inc., 1958), p. 10.

Chapter Five

1. Leo Tolstoy, *A Confession and What I Believe*, trans. Aylmer Maude (London: Oxford University Press, 1921), pp. 23-24.

2. Frederick W. Robertson, *Sermons Preached at Brighton* (New York: Harper & Brothers, n.d.), p. 418.

3. Nicolas Berdyaev, *The Destiny of Man* (New York: Harper Torch books, 1960), p. 252.

4. Helmut Thielicke, *How the World Began*, trans. John W. Doberstein (Philadelphia: Fortress Press, 1961), pp. 177-178.

5. Albert Schweitzer, *Reverence for Life*, trans. Reginald H. Fuller (New York: Harper & Row, 1969), p. 69.

6. Jurgen Moltmann, *Theology of Hope* (New York: Harper & Row, 1967), p. 165.

7. Wolfhart Pannenberg, *The Apostle's Creed in the Light of Today's Questions* (Philadelphia: The Westminster Press, 1972), p. 97.

8. Moltmann, *op. cit.*, p. 166.

9. Carlyle Marney, *Faith in Conflict* (New York: Abingdon Press, 1957), p. 138.

10. Leander E. Keck, "New Testament Views of Death," in *Perspectives on Death*, edited by Liston O. Mills (New York: Abingdon Press, 1969), p. 97.

11. Paul Tillich, *The Shaking of the Foundations* (New York: Charles Scribner's Sons, 1948), p. 159.

12. Lewis Mumford, *The Transformation of Man* (New York: Collier Books, 1956), p. 24.

13. Paul Tillich, *The Shaking of the Foundations* (New York: Charles Scribner's Sons, 1948), p. 83.

14. Emil Brunner, *The Christian Doctrine of the Church, Faith, and the Consummation*, Dogmatics, vol. III, trans. David Cairns (Philadelphia: The Westminster Press, 1960), p. 386.

15. Frank Stagg, *New Testament Theology* (Nashville: Broadman Press, 1962), p. 73.

16. H. Wheeler Robinson, *The Religious Ideas of the Old Testament* (London: Gerald Duckworth & Co., LTD, 1959), p. 85.

17. John Baillie, *And the Life Everlasting* (New York: Charles Scribner's Sons, 1933), p. 163.

18. Stagg, *op. cit.*, p. 326.

19. Emil Brunner, *Eternal Hope*, trans. Harold Knight (London: Lutterworth Press, 1954), p. 152.

20. Karl Barth, *The Resurrection of the Dead*, trans. H. J. Stenning (New York: Fleming H. Revell Co., 1933), p. 169.

21. Brunner, *The Christian Doctrine of the Church*, p. 389.

A Suggested Reading List

Harry Emerson Fosdick. *The Assurance of Immortality*. New York: Association Press, 1918.

John Gunther. *Death Be Not Proud*. New York: Harper & Row, 1949.

Earl A. Grollman (ed.). *Explaining Death to Children*. Boston: Beacon Press, 1967.

Edgar N. Jackson. *Telling a Child About Death*. New York: Hawthorn Books, Inc., 1965.

_____. *Understanding Grief*. Nashville: Abingdon Press, 1957.

_____. *When Someone Dies*. Philadelphia: Fortress Press, 1971.

Bernadine Kreis and Alice Pattie. *Up from Grief*. New York: The Seabury Press, 1969.

Elisabeth Kübler-Ross. *On Death and Dying*. New York: The Macmillan Co., 1969.

C. S. Lewis. *A Grief Observed*. New York: The Seabury Press, 1961.

Elizabeth L. Reed. *Helping Children with the Mystery of Death*. Nashville: Abingdon Press, 1970.

Roger L. Shinn. *Life, Death, and Destiny*. Philadelphia: The Westminster Press, 1957.

Helmut Thielicke. *Death and Life*. Philadelphia: Fortress Press, 1970.

Paul Tournier. *Learn to Grow Old*. New York: Harper & Row, 1972.

Leslie D. Weatherhead. *After Death*. New York: Abingdon Press, n.d.

Granger E. Westberg, *Good Grief*. Philadelphia: Fortress Press, 1962.

H. A. Williams. *True Resurrection*. New York: Holt, Rinehart and Winston, 1972.

Date Due

BP
BROADMAN
SUPPLIES

Code 4386-04, CLS-4, Broadman Supplies, Nashville, Tenn.,
Printed in U.S.A.